John Hely-Hutchinson

The commercial restraints of Ireland considered in a series of letters to a noble lord : containing an historical account of the affairs of that kingdom, so far as they relate to this subject

John Hely-Hutchinson

The commercial restraints of Ireland considered in a series of letters to a noble lord : containing an historical account of the affairs of that kingdom, so far as they relate to this subject

ISBN/EAN: 9783337184803

Printed in Europe, USA, Canada, Australia, Japan

Cover: Foto ©ninafisch / pixelio.de

More available books at **www.hansebooks.com**

THE COMMERCIAL RESTRAINTS OF IRELAND CONSIDERED.

IN A SERIES OF LETTERS TO A NOBLE LORD.

CONTAINING AN HISTORICAL ACCOUNT OF THE AFFAIRS OF THAT KINGDOM, SO FAR AS THEY RELATE TO THIS SUBJECT.

———— *I will awake a higher sense,*
A love that grasps the happiness of millions.
THOMPSON.

DUBLIN:
PRINTED BY WILLIAM HALLHEAD, No. 63, DAME-STREET.
M.DCC.LXXIX.

To the READER.

THE numerous references in thofe letters will, it is hoped, be excufed, when the motive for giving the reader that trouble is confidered. In a fubject of great importance an anonymous writer thought he fhould take too much liberty, in mentioning facts or opinions from himfelf. He

He has therefore reforted to the statute books and journals of parliament in both kingdoms, and to some of the most approved commercial authorities among the English writers. The history of those proceedings seems not to be sufficiently understood in either kingdom; an attempt to collect it from the many journals and acts of parliament, in which it lies dispersed, may possibly assist those who enquire after truth, and wish to form fair and candid conclusions for the good of the whole British Empire. In the consideration of this subject it was necessary

cessary to depart from the chronological order. The great and frequent distresses of Ireland during this century are particularly stated, and carefully examined, through the many different stages of her real poverty and imaginary wealth. From those distresses, as through uniform effects, the causes are traced. The discouragement of the woollen manufactures, by the English act of 1699, as the principal cause, is then considered; the objections arising from the difference of taxes in the two kingdoms removed; and the advantages that must arise to Great Britain

Britain by the repeal of this law stated. It is then shewn that no equivalent was given to Ireland for the loss of the woollen trade; that the encouragement of the linen manufacture was not an equivalent at the time, and if it was, has long ceased to be so. The principle of the act of 1699 is proved not to be justly applicable to Ireland, considered with a view to the natural productions, or to the ancient commercial system of that kingdom; the many English and Irish statutes which established that system are stated down to the year 1663, when the

the commercial restraints first began. Those which arise from the plantation laws, and which began in that year, are then considered, and their effects shewn on the manufacture, commerce, and navigation of Ireland. This system of restraints, if it can be supposed to have been reasonable at the time when it was introduced, is proved to be now ruinous to Ireland and to the British empire.

The advantages over Ireland, which Great Britain possesses in every branch of trade and manufacture, are

are considered in the last place; and it is shewn that if the act of 1699 was repealed, she would still retain a great superiority in the woollen trade. Several of the many other restrictions, under which Ireland labours, are also mentioned.

The discouragement of the woollen manufactures, and the plantation restraints, are principally insisted upon, because they are thought to be the principal cause of its weakness and poverty; but it is not presumed to draw any line on a subject under the consideration of the legi-
slatures

flatures of both kingdoms. Facts are stated, confequences deduced, obfervations made, and the principal grievances are pointed out, the remedies are fubmitted to thofe who have the power to redrefs.

CON-

THE
CONTENTS.

FIRST LETTER.

THE diftrefs of Ireland proved to be great and general.———The temporary caufes of this diftrefs.———There muft be fome permanant caufe, and why   1

SECOND LETTER.

This permanent cause traced from its effects, by considering the state of Ireland at different periods.——From the settlement of Ireland by James, to the year 1641.——From the restoration to the year 1688.——From thence to the year 1699, when the act was passed in England restraining the exportation of all woollen manufactures from Ireland.——In former periods that country advancing in wealth and improvements.——Its poverty and distress from 1699 to the end of Queen Ann's reign.——The woollen manufactures the source of industry in Ireland in 1699, and the discouragement of them the principal cause of this distress.——The same cause continues to operate, and has frequently reduced Ireland to great misery, notwithstanding the encouragement

CONTENTS. xv

ment given by Great Britain to the linen trade.——Its succefs in Ireland 11

THIRD LETTER.

State of Ireland from the death of Queen Ann to the year 1755.———It continued for many years in a low and impoverished state.———Instances in 1716, 1717, 1721, 1723, 1728, 1729, 1731, 1740 and 1741.——Frequent scarcities of corn.———The lower classes of people, in those periods, reduced to great misery.———A small debt, contracted in 1715, increased from time to time, and not paid off until 1754, notwithstanding great œconomy.———From this period the wealth and ability of Ireland overrated, which occasioned increased expences.———The revenue rose from an increase of imports, occasioned by too great a circulation of paper, which gave fictitious credit.———Some of the principal

xvi   CONTENTS.

principal bankers fail in 1754 and 1755.———In thofe years public credit very low, notwithftanding the redundancy in the treafury.———This fuppofed wealth of Ireland the occafion of real poverty   35

FOURTH LETTER.

State of Ireland from 1755 to 1779.——— Revenue fell in 1755, 1756 and 1757. ———Great diftrefs among the poor in the laft mentioned year, and money iffued out of the treafury for their relief.———Army augmented in 1759.——— The efforts made in the war then depending, occafion the failure of fome of the principal bankers, and injure public and private credit.———The wealth of Ireland too highly eftimated.———Encreafe of penfions.———The rupture with Spain occafions a further augmentation of the army in 1761.—
The

CONTENTS. xvii

The risings of the White Boys, which begun in this year, a proof of poverty and want of employment among the lower classes.———— National debt at the peace, contracted during the last war.———— Causes of its encrease.————The lower orders of the people in distress in 1765, 1771, 1778, and 1779.———— No natural or accidental causes for those repeated instances of distress.————They have arisen from mistaken policy   57

FIFTH LETTER.

The English law, prohibiting the exportation of cattle, forced the Irish to encrease their breed of sheep.————The woollen manufacture cultivated for many ages in Ireland.————The exportation from Ireland encouraged by many English and Irish acts.————The addresses of the lords and commons of England, in 1698, not founded on any
      b   prejudice

xviii CONTENTS.

prejudice which the woollen trade of England had received from Ireland.—— The proceedings in that year in England and Ireland upon that subject.—— The report from the commitee of trade. ——Whether the apprehensions of England were well-founded.——The objection arising from the low price of labour and the difference of taxes considered.——If Ireland exported woollen goods, the greatest part of the profit would center in Great Britain.—— Ireland, when ill able, bore a part of the British burthens.——The loss to England by this prohibition.——Petitions and information from trading towns not to be relied upon   83

SIXTH LETTER.

The woollen the principal trade of Ireland in 1699.——The linen not then an equivalent, nor accepted as such. ——The

CONTENTS

The English had, by a statute in 1696, encouraged the linen manufacture in Ireland, without stipulating any restraints.————The linen, if an equivalent for the woollen in 1699, is not so at this time.————Opening the ports of America to Irish white and brown linens, of less value from the restraints of their imports from thence.————Whether the encouragement promised to the linen and hempen manufactures of Ireland has been given.————A populous commercial country cannot be supported by one manufacture.———— Great disadvantages in not having the primum of this manufacture 127

SEVENTH LETTER.

The law of 1699 originated in a system of colonization.————Whether just to bring Ireland within that system.————She was allowed the benefit arising from the colonies

nies till the year 1663.———The commercial fyftem of Ireland ftated from Englifh acts in which Ireland is named, and from the common and ftatute laws of both kingdoms.———In 1663 the diftinctions between the trade of the two kingdoms begun.—Englifh act in that year to prevent exportation from Ireland to the Englifh colonies.———In 1670, act to prevent importation from thence.———This, and the other laws afterwards made for that purpofe, will prevent our having the benefit of the late extenfion of our exports to thofe countries.—Thofe laws confidered.———If this reftrictive fyftem was founded in juftice and good policy in 1663, 1670, and 1699, the prefent ftate of the Britifh empire requires that it fhould be altered   153

EIGHTH LETTER.

The ftate of Ireland at the time of making thofe laws totally different from the prefent.

CONTENTS.

present.———The reasons for making those laws, respecting Ireland, America, England, and foreign countries, have all failed.———A perseverance in this restrictive policy would be now ruinous to Great Britain.——-The great strength and riches which she may acquire from Ireland.———The poverty of Ireland has ever been a drain, and her riches an influx of wealth to England.—Agreement to wear the manufactures of Ireland considered.———Great numbers of people add to the poverty of a nation, if they have not the means of acquiring.———Trade enough for two islands, without distressing the inhabitants of either   191

NINTH LETTER.

Various other prohibitions and restraints give the British trader and manufacturer great advantages over the Irish in every species of trade and manufacture, particularly

cularly in the linen and woollen.—Great Britain would retain great advantages in the latter, though the act of 1699 should be repealed.——Many other restraints on the commerce of Ireland mentioned.——The extension of her commerce would open new sources of trade to the British merchant.——The address of Ireland to her sister kingdom 225

THE COMMERCIAL RESTRAINTS

OF

IRELAND

CONSIDERED.

FIRST LETTER.

THE COMMERCIAL RESTRAINTS OF IRELAND CONSIDERED.

FIRST LETTER.

My Lord,
                   Dublin, 20th Aug. 1779.

YOU defire my thoughts on the affairs of Ireland; a fubject little confidered, and confequently not underftood in England. The Lords and Commons of Great Britain have addreffed his Majefty to take the diftreffed and impoverifhed ftate of this country into confideration; have called for information, and refolved to purfue effectual methods for promoting the common ftrength, wealth and commerce of both kingdoms; and his Majefty has been pleafed to exprefs, in his fpeech from the throne, his entire approbation of their attention to the present state of Ireland.

The occasion calls for the assistance of every friend to the British empire: those who can give material information are bound to communicate it. The attempt however is full of difficulty; it will require more than ordinary caution to write with such moderation as not to offend the prejudices of one country, and with such freedom as not to wound the feelings of the other.

The present state of Ireland teems with every circumstance of national poverty. Whatever the land produces is greatly reduced in its value: wool is fallen one half in its usual price; wheat one third; black cattle of all kinds in the same proportion, and hides in a much greater: buyers are not had without difficulty at those low rates, and from the principal fairs men commonly return with the commodities they brought there: rents are every where reduced, in many places it is impossible to collect them:
the

LET. I.   OF IRELAND CONSIDERED.   5

the farmers are all diftreffed, and many of them have failed: when leafes expire, tenants are not eafily found: the landlord is often obliged to take his lands into his own hands, for want of bidders at reafonable rents, and finds his eftate fallen one fourth in its value. The merchant juftly complains that all bufinefs is at a ftand, that he cannot difcount his bills, and that neither money nor paper circulates. In this and the laft year, above twenty thoufand manufacturers, in this metropolis, were reduced to beggary for want of employment; they were for a confiderable length of time fupported by alms; a part of the contribution came from England, and this affiftance was much wanting from the general diftrefs of all ranks of people in this country. Public and private credit are annihilated: parliament, that always raifes money in Ireland on eafy terms, when there is any to be borrowed in the country, in 1778 gave 7½l. per cent. in annuities, which in 1773 and 1775 were earneftly fought after at 6l. then thought to be a very high rate. The expences of a country, nearly bankrupt,

muft

must be inconsiderable; almost every branch of the revenue has fallen; and the receipts in the treasury for the two years, ending lady-day, 1779, were less than those for the two years, ending lady-day, 1777, deducting the sums received on account of loans in each period, in a sum of 334,900l. 18s. 9½d.: there was due on the 25th of March last, on the establishments, and for extraordinary expences, an arrear amounting to 373,706l. 13s. 6½d.: a sum of 600,000l. will probably be now wanting to supply the deficiencies on the establishments and extraordinary charges of government: and an annual sum of between 50 and 60,000l. yearly, to pay interest and annuities: in the last session 466,000l. was borrowed; if the sum wanting could now be raised, the debt would be increased in a sum of above 1,000,000l. in less than three years, and if the expences and the revenues should continue the same as in the last two years, there is a probability of an annual deficiency of 300,000l. The nation in the last two years has not been able to pay for its own defence; a militia law,

LET. I.   OF IRELAND CONSIDERED.   7

law, paſſed in the laſt ſeſſion, could not be carried into execution for want of money. Inſtead of paying forces abroad *, Ireland has not been able in this year to pay the forces kept in the kingdom: it has again relapſed into its ancient ſtate of imbecility, and Great Britain has been lately obliged to ſend over money to pay the army † which defends this impoveriſhed country.

Our diſtreſs and poverty are of the utmoſt notoriety; the proof does not depend ſolely upon calculation or eſtimate, it is palpable in every public and private tranſaction, and is deeply felt among all orders of our people.

This kingdom has been long declining. The annual deficiency of its revenues for the payment of the public expences, has been, for many years, ſupplied by borrowing.

* On account of the inability of Ireland, Great Britain ſince Chriſtmas, 1778, relieved her from the burden of paying forces abroad.

† A ſum of 50,000l. has been lately ſent from England for that purpoſe.

ing. The American rebellion, which considerably diminished the demand for our linens; an embargo on provisions continued for three years*, and highly injurious to our victualling trade; the increasing drain of remittances to England for rents, salaries, profits of offices, pensions and interest, and for the payment of forces abroad, have made the decline more rapid, but have not occasioned it.

If we are determined to investigate the truth, we must assign a more radical cause: when the human or political body is unsound or infirm, it is in vain to inquire what accidental circumstances appear to have occasioned those maladies which arise from the constitution itself.

If

---

* By a Proclamation, dated the 3d of February, 1776, on all ships and vessels, laden in any of the ports in this kingdom, with provisions of any kind, but not to extend to ships carrying salted beef, pork, butter and bacon into Great Britain, or provisions to any part of the British empire, except the Colonies mentioned in the said proclamation. 4th of January, 1779, taken off as far as it relates to ships carrying provisions to any of the ports of Europe.

LET. I. OF IRELAND CONSIDERED.

If in a period of fourscore years of profound internal peace, any country shall appear to have often experienced the extremes of poverty and distress; if at the times of her greatest supposed affluence and prosperity, the slightest causes have been sufficient to obstruct her progress, to annihilate her credit, and to spread dejection and dismay among all ranks of her people ; and if such a country is blessed with a temperate climate and fruitful soil, abounds with excellent harbours and great rivers, with the necessaries of life and materials of manufacture, and is inhabited by a race of men, brave, active and intelligent, some permanent cause of such disastrous effects must be sought for.

If your vessel is frequently in danger of foundering in the midst of a calm; if by the smallest addition of sail she is near oversetting, let the gale be ever so steady, you would neither reproach the crew, nor accuse the pilot or the master ; you would look to the construction of the vessel, and see how she had been originally framed, and whether any new works had been added

added to her, that retard or endanger her course.

But for such an examination more time and attention are necessary than have been usually bestowed upon this subject in Great Britain; and as I have now the honour to address a person of rank and station in that kingdom on the affairs of Ireland, I should be brief in my first audience, or I may happen never to obtain the favour of a second.

I have the honour to be, my lord, &c.

THE
COMMERCIAL RESTRAINTS
OF
IRELAND
CONSIDERED.

SECOND LETTER.

THE COMMERCIAL RESTRAINTS OF IRELAND CONSIDERED.

SECOND LETTER.

My Lord,

Dublin, 23d August, 1779.

IF there is any such permanent cause, from which the frequent distresses of so considerable a part of the British empire have arisen, it is of the utmost consequence that it should be fully explained, and generally understood. Let us endeavour to trace it by its effects; these will manifestly appear by an attentive review of the state of Ireland at different periods.

From the time that king James the First had established a regular administration of justice

justice in every part of the kingdom, until the rebellion of 1641, which takes in a period of between thirty and forty years, the growth of Ireland was considerable *. In the act recognizing the title of king James, the Lords and Commons acknowledge " that many blessings and benefits had, " within these few years past, been poured " upon this realm † ;" and at the end of the parliament in 1615, the commons return thanks for the extraordinary pains taken for the good of this republic, whereby they say " we all of us sit under our own vines, " and the whole realm reapeth the happy " fruits of peace ‡." In his reign the little that could be given by the people, was given with general consent § : and received with extraordinary marks of royal favour; he

---

* Its tranquillity was so well established in 1611, that king James reduced his army in Ireland to 176 horse, and 1450 foot. Additional judges were appointed; circuits established throughout the kingdom, 2d Cox, 17 ; and Sir John Davis observes, that no nation under the sun loves equal and indifferent justice better than the Irish. Davis, p. 184, 196.

† 13 Jac. ch. i.   ‡ 1 Vol. Com. Journ. p. 92.
§ Ib. 61.

he desires the lord-deputy to return them thanks for their subsidy, and for their granting it with universal consent*; and to assure them that he holds his subjects of that kingdom in equal favour with those of his other kingdoms; and that he will be as careful to provide for their prosperous and flourishing state, as for his own person.

Davis, who had served him in great stations in this kingdom, and had visited every province of it, mentions the prosperous state of the country, and that the revenue of the crown, both certain and casual, had been raised to a double proportion. He takes notice how this was effected, " by the " encouragement given to the maritime " towns and cities, as well to increase the " trade of merchandize, as to cherish me- " chanical arts;" and mentions the consequence, " that the strings of this Irish harp " were all in tune †."

In

---

* 1 Vol. Com. Journ. p. 88.
† Davis, p. 1, 193, 194.

In the succeeding reign, Ireland for fourteen or fifteen years appears to have greatly advanced in prosperity. The commons granted in the session of 1634, six entire subsidies, which they agreed should amount in the collection to 250,000l.*; and the free gifts previously given to king Charles the First, at different times, amounted to 310,000l. †; in the session of 1639, they gave four entire subsidies, and the clergy eight; the customs which had been farmed at 500l. yearly, in the beginning of this reign, were in the progress of it set for 54,000l. ‡

The commodities exported were twice as much in value, as the foreign merchandize imported, and shipping is said to have increased an hundred fold §. Their parliament was encouraged to frame laws conducive

---

* Cox's Hist. of Ireland, 2 Vol. 61. † Ib.
† Some of these subsides, from the subsequent times of confusion, were not raised.
‡ Cox, 2d Vol. p. 33.
§ Leland's Hist. of Ireland, 3d Vol. p. 41.

cive to the happiness and prosperity of themselves and their posterities, for the enacting and "consummating" whereof the king passes his royal word; and assures his subjects of Ireland that they were equally of as much respect and dearness to him as any others *.

In the speaker's speech in 1639, when he was offered for approbation to the lord-deputy, he mentions the free and happy condition of the people of Ireland; sets forth the particulars; and in enumerating the national blessings, mentions as one, " that our in-gates and out-gates do stand open for trade and traffic †;" and as the lord chancellor declared his excellency's " high liking of this oration," it may be considered as a fair account of the condition of Ireland at that time. When the commons had afterwards caught the infection of the times, and were little disposed to pay

com-

---

* Lord Strafford's Letters, 2d Vol. p. 297.
† Ir. Com. Journ. 1st Vol. p. 228, 229.

compliments, they acknowledge, that this kingdom, when the earl of Strafford obtained the government, " was in a flourishing, " wealthy and happy estate *."

After the restoration, from the time that the acts of settlement and explanation had been fully carried into execution, to the year 1688, Ireland made great advances, and continued, for several years, in a most prosperous condition †. Lands were every where improved; rents were doubled; the kingdom abounded with money; trade flourished to the envy of our neighbours; cities increased exceedingly; many places of the kingdom

* Lord Clarendon. Cox, ib. Ir. Com. Journ. 1 Vol. p. 280, 311.

† Archbishop King, in his State of the Protestants of Ireland, p. 52, 53, 445, 446. Lord Chief Justice Keating's Address to James the Second, and his Letter to Sir John Temple, ib.

The prohibition of the exportation of our cattle to England, though a great, was but a temporary distress; and in its consequences greatly promoted the general welfare of this country.

kingdom equalled the improvements of England; the king's revenue increased proportionably to the advance of the kingdom, which was every day growing, and was *well established in plenty and wealth* *; manufactures were set on foot in divers parts; the meanest inhabitants were at once enriched and civilized: and this kingdom is then represented to be the most improved and improving spot of ground in Europe. I repeat the words of persons of high rank, great character and superior knowledge, who could not be deceived themselves, and were incapable of deceiving others.

In the former of these periods, parliaments were seldom convened in Ireland; in the latter, they were suspended for the space of twenty-six years; during that time the English ministers frequently shewed dispositions unfavourable to the prosperity of this kingdom; and in the interval between

---

* Lord Sydney's words in his speech from the throne, in 1692, from his own former knowledge of this country. Ir. Com. Journ. 2d Vol. p. 577.

between thofe two periods, it had been laid wafte, and almoft depopulated by civil rage and religious fury. And yet, after being bleffed with an internal peace of ninety years, and with a fucceffion of five excellent fovereigns, who were moft juftly the objects of our affection and gratitude, and to whom the people of this country were defervedly dear; after fo long and happy an intercourfe of protection grace and favour from the crown, and of duty and loyalty from the fubjects, it would be difficult to find any fubfequent period where fo flattering a view has been given of the induftry and profperity of Ireland.

The caufe of this profperity fhould be mentioned. James, the firft duke of Ormond, whofe memory fhould be ever revered by every friend of Ireland, to heal the wound that this country had received by the prohibition of the export of her cattle to England, obtained from Charles the Second a letter [*], dated the 23d of March 1667, by which

[*] Carte, 2 Vol. p. 342, 344.

which he directed that all reſtraints upon the exportation of commodities, of the growth or manufacture of Ireland, to foreign parts, ſhould be taken off, but not to interfere with the plantation laws, or the charters to the trading companies, and that this ſhould be notified to his ſubjects of this kingdom; which was accordingly done by a proclamation from the lord lieutenant and council; and at the ſame time, by his majeſty's permiſſion, they prohibited the importation from Scotland of linen, woollen, and other manufactures and commodities, as drawing large ſums of money out of Ireland, and a great hindrance to its manufactures. His grace ſuccefsfully executed his ſchemes of national improvement, having by his own conſtant attention, the exertion of his extenſive influence, and the moſt princely munificence, greatly advanced the woollen, and revived § the linen manufactures, which England

§ Lord Strafford laid the foundation of the linen manufacture in Ireland, but the troubles which ſoon after broke out had entirely ſtopped the progreſs of it.

England then encouraged in this kingdom, as a compenfation for the lofs of that trade of which fhe had deprived; it and this encouragement, from that time to the revolution, had greatly increafed the wealth and promoted the improvement of Ireland.

The tyranny and perfecuting policy of James the fecond † after his arrival in Ireland, ruined its trade and revenue; the many great oppreffions which the people fuffered during the revolution had occafioned almoft the *utter defolation* of the country. § But the nation muft have been reftored in the reign of William to a confiderable degree of ftrength and vigor: their exertions in raifing fupplies to a great amount, from the year 1692 to the year 1698, are fome proof of it. They taxed their goods, their lands, their perfons, in fupport of a prince whom they juftly called their deliverer and defender, and

† Harris's Life of K. W. 116.
§ The Words of Lord Sydney, in his fpeech from the throne in 1692. Com. Jour. 2 Vol. 576.

and of a government on which their own preservation depended. Those sums were granted †, not only without murmur, but with the utmost chearfulness, and without any complaint of the inability, or representation of the distressed state of the country.

The money brought in for the army at the revolution, gave life to all business, and much sooner than could have been expected retrieved the affairs of Ireland. This money furnished capitals for carrying on the manufactures of the kingdom. Our exports increased in 96, 97 and 98, and our imports did not rise in proportion, which occasioned a great balance in our favour; and this increase was owing principally to the woollen manufacture. In the last of those years the ballance in favour of Ireland in the account of exports and imports was 419,442l §.

But in the latter end of this reign the political horizon was overcast, the national growth was checked, and the national vigor and industry

† Ir. Com. Jour. 3 Vol. 45 and 65, that great supplies were given during this period. § Dobbs, p. 5, 6, 7, 19.

dustry impaired by the law made in England, restraining, in fact prohibiting the exportation of all woollen manufactures from Ireland. From the time of this prohibition no parliament was held in Ireland until the year 1703. Five years were suffered to pass before any opportunity was given to apply a remedy to the many evils which such a prohibition must necessarily have occasioned. The linen-trade was then not thoroughly established in Ireland; the woollen manufacture was the staple trade, and wool the principal material of that kingdom. The consequences of this prohibition appear in the session of 1703 †. The commons § lay before queen Anne a most affecting representation, containing, to use their own words "a true state of our deplorable condition," protesting that no groundless discontent was the motive for that application, but a deep sense of the evil state of their country, and of the farther mischiefs they have reason to fear will fall

† Com. Jour. 3 Vol. 45.
§ Ir. Com. Jour. 3 Vol. 65, 66.

fall upon it, if not timely prevented. They set forth the vaſt decay and loſs of its trade, its being almoſt exhauſted of coin, that they are hindered from earning their livelihoods, and from maintaining their own manufactures, that their poor are thereby become very numerous; that great numbers of proteſtant families have been conſtrained to remove out of the kingdom, as well into Scotland as into the dominions of foreign princes and ſtates, and that their foreign trade and its returns are under ſuch reſtrictions and diſcouragements as to be then become in a manner impracticable, although that kingdom had by its blood and treaſure contributed to ſecure the plantation trade to the people of England.

In a further addreſs to the queen*, laid before the duke of Ormond, then lord lieutenant, by the houſe with its ſpeaker, they mention the diſtreſſed condition of that kingdom, and more eſpecially of the induſtrious
proteſtants,

---

* Com. Jour. 3 Vol. 149.

protestants, by the almost total loss of trade and decay of their manufactures, and to preserve the country from utter ruin, apply for liberty to export their linen manufactures to the plantations.

In a subsequent part of this session *, the commons resolve, that by reason of the great decay of trade and discouragement of the manufactures of this kingdom, many poor tradesmen were reduced to extreme want and beggary. This resolution was *nem. con.* and the speaker, Mr. Broderick, then his majesty's solicitor general, and afterwards lord chancellor, in his speech at the end of the session†, informs the lord lieutenant, that the representation of the commons was, as to the matters contained in it, the unanimous voice and consent of a very full house, and that the soft and gentle terms used by the commons in laying the distressed condition of the kingdom before his majesty, shewed that their complaints proceeded not from querulousness, but

* Ir. Com. Jour. 3 Vol. p. 195.   Ib. 207, 208.

but from a neceffity of feeking redrefs; he adds, "it is to be hoped they may be al-
"lowed fuch a proportion of trade, that
"they may recover from the great poverty
"they now lie under;" and in prefenting the bill of fupply fays, the commons have granted it " in time of extreme poverty." The impoverifhed ftate of Ireland, at that time, appears in the fpeech from the throne at the conclufion of the feffion, in which it is mentioned that the commons could not then provide for what was owing to the civil and military lifts*.

The fupply given for two years, commencing at Michaelmas 1703 †, was a fum not exceeding 150,000l. which, confidering that no parliament was held in Ireland fince the year 1698, is at the rate of 30,000l.—— yearly commencing in 1699, and ending in the year 1705.

The great diftrefs of Ireland, from the year 1699, to the year 1703, and the caufe of that diftrefs, cannot be doubted.

Let

* Com. Jour. 3 Vol. p. 210.   † Ib. 79, 94.

Let it now be confidered, whether the fame caufe has operated fince the year 1703. In the year 1704* it appears, that the commons were not able, from the circumftances of the nation at that time, to make provifion for repairing the neceffary fortifications; or for arms and ammunition for the public fafety: and the difficulties which the kingdom then laboured under, and the decay of trade appear by the addreffes of the commons† to the queen, and to the duke of Ormond, then lord lieutenant, who was well acquainted with the ftate of this country; by the queen's anfwer‡, and the addrefs of thanks for it.

In the year 1707 §, the revenue was deficient for payment of the army, and defraying the charges of government; and the commons promife to fupply the deficiency "as far as the prefent circumftances of the "nation will allow."

In

* Com. Jour. 3 Vol. p. 298.   † Ib. 225, 266.
‡ Ib. 253, 258.   § Ib. 364, 368, 369.

In 1709, it appears * by the unanimous address of the commons to the lord lieutenant, that the kingdom was in an impoverished and exhausted state: in 1711 †, they express their approbation of the frugality of the queen's administration, by which their expences were lessened, and by that means the kingdom preserved from taxes, which might have proved too weighty and burthensome. In their addrefs to the lord lieutenant, at the close of the session, they request, that he should represent to her majesty, that they had given all the supplies which her majesty desired, and which they, in their present condition, were able to grant ‡: and yet those supplies amounted, for two years, to a sum not exceeding 167,023l. 8s. 5d §; though powder magazines, the council chamber, the treasury office, and other offices were then to be built.

From the short parliament of 1713, nothing can be collected, but that the house was

* Com. Jour. 3 Vol. p. 573.   † Ib. 827.   ‡ Ib. 929.
§ Ib. 876.

was inflamed and divided by party diffentions, and that the fear of danger to the succeffion of the prefent illuftrious family, excluded every other confideration from the minds of the majority.

This laft period, from the year 1699 to the death of queen Anne, is marked with the ftrongeft circumftances of national diftrefs and defpondency. The reprefentatives of the people, who were the beft judges, and feveral of whom were members of the houfe of commons before and after thefe reftraints, have affigned the reafon. No other can be affigned.

That the woollen manufactures were the great fource of induftry in Ireland, appears from the Irifh ftatute of the 17th and 18th of Charles II. ch. 15[*]; from the refolutions

[*] In the fame feffion an act was made for the advancement of the linen manufacture, which fhews that both kingdoms then thought (for thefe laws came to us through England) that each of thefe manufactures was to be encouraged in Ireland.

solutions of the commons in 1695*, for regulating those manufactures; the resolutions of the committee of supply in that session†; and from the preamble to the English statute of the 10th and 11th of William III. ch. 10; in which it is recited, that great quantities of those manufactures were made, and were daily increasing in Ireland, and were exported from thence to foreign markets.

Of the exportation of all those manufactures the Irish were at once totally deprived: the linen manufacture, proposed as a substitute, must have required the attention of many years before it could be thoroughly established. What must have been the consequences to Ireland in the mean time? the journals of the commons in queen Anne's reign have informed us. Compare this period with the three former, and you will prove this melancholy truth; that a country

* Ir. Com. Jour. 2 Vol. p. 725. † Ib. 733.

try will sooner recover from the miseries and devastation occasioned by war, invasion, rebellion, massacre, than from laws restraining the commerce, discouraging the manufactures, fettering the industry, and above all breaking the spirits of the people.

It would be injustice not to acknowledge that Great Britain has, for a long series of years, made great exertions to repair the evils arising from these restraints. She has opened her great markets to part of the linen manufacture of Ireland; she has encouraged it by granting, for a great length of time, large sums of her own money † on the exportation of it; and under her protection, and by the persevering industry of our people, this manufacture has attained to a great degree of perfection and prosperity, in some parts of this country. If the kind and constant attention of that great kingdom,

with

† The sums paid on the exportation of Irish linens from Great Britain, at a medium of twenty-nine years, from 1743 to 1773, amount to something under 10,000l. yearly.—Ir. Com. Jour. 16 Vol. p. 374, the account returned from the inspector general's office in Great Britain.

LET. 2.   OF IRELAND CONSIDERED.

with which we are connected to this important object; or if the lenient courfe of time had at length healed thofe wounds, which commercial jealoufy had given to the trade and induftry of this country, it would not be a friendly hand to either kingdom that would attempt to open them: but, if upon every accident they bleed anew, they fhould be carefully examined, and fearched to the bottom. If the caufe of the poverty and diftrefs of Ireland in the reign of queen Anne has fince continued to operate, though not always in fo great a degree, yet fufficient frequently to reduce to mifery, and conftantly to check the growth and impair the ftrength of that kingdom, and to weaken the force and to reduce the refources of Great Britain; that man ought to be confidered as a friend to the Britifh empire, who endeavours to eftablifh this important truth, and to explain a fubject fo little underftood. If in this attempt there fhall appear no intention to raife jealoufies, inflame difcontents, or agitate conftitutional queftions, it is hoped that thofe letters may be be read without prejudice on one side of the water, and without passion or resentment on the other.

I have the honour to be, my lord, &c.

THE

COMMERCIAL RESTRAINTS

OF

IRELAND

CONSIDERED.

THIRD LETTER.

THE COMMERCIAL RESTRAINTS

OF

IRELAND

CONSIDERED.

THIRD LETTER.

My Lord,

Dublin, 25th August, 1779.

To an inquirer after truth, hiftory fince the year 1699 furnifhes very imperfect and often partial views of the affairs of Great Britain and Ireland. The latter has no profeffed hiftorian of its own fince that æra, and is fo flightly mentioned in the hiftories of the former kingdom, that it feems to be introduced rather to fhew the accuracy of the accomptant, than as an article to be read and examined; pamphlets are often written to ferve occafional purpofes, and with an intention to mifreprefent; and party writers

ters are not worthy of any regard. We must then endeavour to find some other guide, and look into the best materials for history, by considering the facts as recorded in the journals of parliament; these have evinced the poverty of Ireland for the first fourteen years of this century. That this poverty continued in the year 1716, appears by the unanimous address of the house of commons to George the First*. This address was to congratulate his majesty on his success in extinguishing the rebellion, an occasion most joyful to them, and on which no disagreeable circumstance would have been stated, had not truth and the necessities of their country extorted it from them. A small debt of 16,106l. 11s. 0½d. †, due at Michaelmas 1715, was, by their exertions to strengthen the hands of government in that year, increased at Midsummer 1717 to a sum of 91537l. 17s. 1⅜d. §, which was considered as such an augmentation of the national

---

* Com. Jour. 4 Vol. p. 249,   † Ib. 296.
§ Ib. 335.

tional debt, that the lord lieutenant, the duke of Bolton, thought it neceffary to take notice in his fpeech from the throne, that the debt was confiderably augmented, and to declare at the fame time that his majefty had ordered reductions in the military, and had thought proper to leffen the civil lift.

There cannot be a ftronger proof of the want of refources in any country, than that a debt of fo fmall an amount fhould alarm the perfons intrufted with the government of it. That thofe apprehenfions were well founded, will appear from the repeated diftreffes of Ireland, from time to time, for many years afterwards. In 1721, the fpeech from the throne*, and the addreffes to the king and to the lord lieutenant, ftate, in the ftrongeft terms, the great decay of her trade, and the very low and impoverifhed ftate to which fhe was reduced.

That

---

* Com. Jour. 4 Vol. p. 694, 700, 701.

That this proceeded, in fome meafure, from calamities and misfortunes which affected the neighbouring kingdoms, is true: but their effects on Ireland, little interefted in the South Sea project, could not be confiderable. The poverty under which fhe laboured, arofe principally from her own fituation: The lord lieutenant fays there is ground to hope that in this feffion fuch remedies may be applied, as will reftore the nation to a flourifhing condition; and the commons return the king thanks for giving them that opportunity to confider of the beft methods for reviving their decayed trade, and making them a flourifhing and happy people.

But it is a melancholy proof of the defponding ftate of this kingdom, that no law whatever was then propofed for encouraging trade or manufactures, or to follow the words of the addrefs, for reviving trade, or making us a flourifhing people, unlefs that for amending the laws as to butter and tallow cafks deferves to be fo called; and why? becaufe it

was

was well underſtood by both houſes of parliament that they had no power to remove thoſe reſtraints which prohibited trade and diſcouraged manufactures, and that any application for that purpoſe would at that time have only offended the people on one ſide of the channel, without bringing any relief to thoſe on the other. The remedy propoſed by government, and partly executed, by directing a commiſſion under the great ſeal for receiving voluntary ſubſcriptions*, in order to eſtabliſh a bank, was a ſcheme to circulate paper without money; and conſidering that it came ſo ſoon after the ſouth ſea bubble had burſt, it is more ſurpriſing that it ſhould have been at firſt applauded †, than that it was in the ſame ſeſſion diſliked, cenſured and abandoned §. The total inefficacy of the remedy proved however the inveteracy of the diſeaſe, and furniſhes a farther proof of the deſperate ſituation of Ireland, when nothing could be thought of for its relief, but that

* Ir. Com. Jour. 4 Vol. p. 694.   † Ib. 720.
§ Ib. 832.

that paper should circulate without money, trade or manufactures *.

In the following session of 1723, it appears that the condition of our manufacturers, and of the lowest classes of our people, must have been distressed, as the duke of Grafton, in his speech from the throne, particularly recommends to their consideration the finding out of some method for the better employing of the poor †; and though the debt of the nation was no more than 66,318l. 8s. 3½d. ‡ and was less than in the *last* session §, yet the commons thought it necessary to present an address to the king, to give such directions as he, in his great goodness should think proper, to prevent the increase of the debt of the nation. This address was presented ‖ by the house, with its

---

* It is not here intended to enter into the question, whether in different circumstances a national bank might not be useful to Ireland.
† Com. Jour. 5 Vol. p. 12. ‡ 5 Vol. p. 102.
§ It was then 77,261l. 6s. 7 d. 4 Vol. p. 778.
‖ Ib. 108.

its speaker, and passed *nem. con.* and was occasioned by the distressed state of the country, and by their apprehensions that it might be further exhausted by the project of Woods's half-pence: it could not be meant as any want of respect to their lord lieutenant, as they had not long since returned him thanks for his wise conduct and frugality in not increasing the debt of the nation*; this address of the commons, and the lord lieutenant's recommendation for the better employing the poor, seems to be explained by a petition of the woollen-drapers, weavers and clothiers of the city of Dublin, (the principal seat of the woollen manufacture of Ireland) in behalf of themselves and the other drapers, weavers and clothiers of this kingdom, praying relief in relation to the great decay of trade in the woollen manufacture †.

But this address had no effect; the debt of the nation in the ensuing session of 1725, was

---

Com. Jour. 4 Vol. p. 16.   † Ib. 136.

was nearly doubled*; in the speeches from the throne in 1727, Lord Carteret takes notice of our success in the linen trade, and yet observes in 1729, that the revenue had fallen short, and that thereby a considerable arrear was due to the establishment.

But notwithstanding the success of the linen manufacture †, Ireland was in a most miserable condition. The great scarcity of corn had been so universal in this kingdom in the years 1728 and 1729, as to expose thousands of families to the utmost necessities, and even to the danger of famine; many artificers and house-keepers having been obliged to beg for bread in the streets of Dublin. It appeared before the house of commons that the import of corn for one year and six months, ending the 29th day of September, 1729, amounted in value to the sum of 274,000l. an amazing sum compared with the circumstances of the kingdom

at

---

* At midsummer, 1725, it amounted to 119,215l. 5s. 3½d. 5 Vol. Com. Jour. p. 282, 295. Ib. 434, 435, 642.
† Ib. 732, 755.

at that time! and the commons refolve that public granaries would greatly contribute to the increafing of tillage, and providing againft fuch wants as have frequently befallen the people of this kingdom, and hereafter may befall them, unlefs proper precautions fhall be taken againft fo great a calamity.

The great fcarcity which happened in the years 28 and 29, and frequently before and fince, is a decifive proof that the diftreffes of this kingdom have been occafioned by the difcouragement of manufactures; if the manufacturers have not fufficient employment they cannot buy the fuperfluous produce of the land; the farmers will be difcouraged from tilling, and general diftrefs and poverty muft enfue. The confequences of the want of employment among manufacturers and labourers muft be more fatal in Ireland than in moft other countries; of the numbers of her people it has been computed that 1,887,220 live in houfes with but one hearth, and may therefore be reafonably prefumed presumed to belong, for the most part, to those classes.

In the year 1731 * there was a great deficiency in the public revenue, and the national debt had considerably increased. The exhausted kingdom lay under great difficulties by the decay of trade, the scarcity of money and the universal poverty of the country, which the speaker represents § in very affecting terms, in offering the money-bills for the royal assent, and adds, "that the com-
" mons hope from his majesty's goodness,
" and his grace's *free* and *impartial* represen-
" tation of the state and condition of this
" kingdom, that *they* may enjoy a *share* of
" the blessings of public tranquillity, by the
" increase of their trade and the encourage-
" ment of their manufactures."

But in the next session, of 1733, they are told in the speech from the throne, what this share was to be. The lord lieutenant informs

* Duke of Dorset's speech from the throne, **Com. Jour,** 6 Vol. p. 12.   § Ib. 143.

forms them that the peace cannot fail of contributing to their welfare, by enabling them to improve thofe branches of trade and manufactures † which *are properly their own,* meaning the trade and manufacture of linen. Whether this idea of property has been preferved inviolate will hereafter appear.

The years 40 and 41 were feafons of great fcarcity, and in confequence of the want of wholefome provifions great numbers of our people perifhed miferably, and the fpeech from the throne recommends it to both houfes to confider of proper meafures to prevent the like calamity for the future. The employment of the poor and the encouragement of tillage, are the remedies propofed § by the lord lieutenant and approved of by the commons, but no laws for thofe purpofes were introduced, and why they were not affords matter for melancholy conjecture. They could not have been infenfible of the miferies of their fellow-creatures; many thoufands

† Com. Jour. 6 v. 189.
§ 7 V. Com. Jour. 214, 220, 222.

thousands of whom were lost in those years, some from absolute want, and many from disorders occasioned by bad provisions. Why was no attempt made for their relief? because the commons knew that the evil was out of their reach, that the poor were not employed because they were discouraged by restrictive laws from working up the materials of their own country, and that agriculture could not be encouraged where the lower classes of the people were not enabled by their industry to purchase the produce of the farmer's labour.

For above forty years after making those restrictive laws * Ireland was always poor and often in great want, distress and misery, § tho' the linen manufacture had made great progress during that time. In the war before the last, she was not able to give any assistance. The duke of Devonshire, in the year 1741, takes

* The act intitled an act for better regulation of partnerships, and to encourage the trade and manufactures of this kingdom, has not a word relative to the latter part of the title.

§ Com. Jour. 6 v. 694, 7 v. 742.

takes notice from the throne, that during a war for the protection of the trade of all his majesty's dominions there had been no increase of the charge of the establishment; and in the year 1745 the country was so little able to bear expence, that lord Chesterfield discouraged and prevented any augmentation of the army, tho' much desired by many gentlemen of the house of commons, from a sense of the great danger that then impended. An influx of money after the peace, and the further success of the linen trade, encreased our wealth, and enabled us to reduce by degrees, and afterwards to discharge the national debt. This was not effected until the first of March 1754*. This debt was occasioned principally by the expences incurred by the rebellion in Great Britain in the year 1715; an unlimited vote

* The sum remaining due on the loans at lady-day 1753 was 85,585l. 0s 9½d The whole credit of the nation to that day was 332,747l. 19s 1½d and, deducting the sums due on the loans, amounted to 247,162l. 18s 3½d. Com. Jour. 9 v. 3, 349, 352.

of credit was then given §. From the lowness of the revenue, and the want of resources, not from any further exertions on the part of the kingdom in point of expence, the debt of 16,106l 11s 0½d due in 1715, was encreased at Lady Day† 1733, to 371,312l 12s 2½d. That government and the house of commons should for such a length of time have considered the reduction and discharge of this debt as an object of so great importance, and that near forty years should have passed, before the constant attention and strictest œconomy of both could have accomplished that purpose, is a strong proof of the weakness and poverty of this country, during that period.

After the payment of this debt, the wealth and ability of Ireland were greatly overrated, both here and in Great Britain. The consequences of this mistaken opinion were encreased expences on the part of government

§ Com. Jour. vol. 4. 195.
† Com. Jour, vol. 6. 289.

ment and of the country, more than it was able to bear. The strict œconomy of old times was no longer practised. The representatives of the people set the example of profusion, and the ministers of the crown were not backward in following it. A large redundency of money in the treasury, gave a delusive appearance of national wealth. At Lady Day 1755 the sum in credit to the nation was 471,404l 5s 6d¾ ‖, and the money remaining in the treasury of the ordinary unappropriated revenue on the 29th day of September 1755*, 457,959l 12s 7d½. But this great increase of revenue arose from an increase of imports, particularly in the year 1754, by which the kingdom was greatly overstocked, and which raised the revenue in that year 208,309l 19s 2d¼ higher than it was in the year 1748, when the revenue first began to rise considerably †; and though what a nation spends is one method of estimating its wealth, yet a nation, like an individual,

‖ Com. Jour. 9 v. 352.   * Ib. 352.
† Com. Jour. 10 Vol. 751.

vidual, may live beyond its means, and spend on credit which may far exceed its income. This was the fact as to Ireland in the year 1754, for some years before and for many years after; it appeared in an enquiry before the house of commons in the session of 1755, that many persons had circulated paper to a very great amount, far exceeding not only their own capitals*, but that just proportion which the quantity of paper ought to bear to the national specie. This gave credit to many individuals, who without property became merchant importers, and at the same time increased the receipts of the treasury and lessened the wealth of the kingdom. At the very time that so great a balance was in the treasury, public credit was in a very low way, and the house of commons was employed in preparing a law to restore it. In 54 and 55 three principal banks‡ had failed,

---

* Com. Jour. 9 v. 818. † Ib. 819, 829, 846, 865.
‡ March 6, 1754, Thomas Dillon and Richard Ferral, failed. 3d March 1755, William Lennox and George French. Same day John Wilcocks and John Dawson.

failed and the legiflature took up much time in enquiring into their affairs, and in framing laws for the relief of their creditors §. Yet in this feffion, the liberality of the houfe of commons was exceffive. The redundency in the treafury had in the feffion of 1753, occafioned a difpute between the crown and the houfe of commons on the queftion, whether the king's previous confent was neceffary for the application of it. They wifhed to avoid any future conteft of that kind, and were flattered to grant the public money from enlarged views of national improvements. The making rivers navigable, the making and improving harbours, and the improvement of hufbandry and other ufeful arts, were objects worthy of the reprefentatives of the people; and had the faithfulnefs of the execution anfwered the goodnefs of the intention in many inftances, the public in general might have had no great reafon to complain. Many of thofe grants prove the poverty of the country.

There

§ There was then no Bankruptcy law in Ireland.

There were not private stocks to carry on the projects of individuals, nor funds sufficient for incorporating and supporting companies, nor profits to be had by the undertakings sufficient to reimburse the money necessary to be expended. The commons therefore advanced the money, for the benefit of the public; and it can never be supposed that they would have continued to do so for above twenty years, if they were not convinced that there were not funds in the hands of individuals sufficient to carry on those useful undertakings, nor trade enough in the kingdom to make adequate returns to the adventurers.

Having gone through more than half the century, it is time to pause. In this long gloomy period, the poverty of Ireland appears to have been misery and desolation, and her wealth a symptom of decline and a prelude to poverty; the low retiring ebb from the spring-tide of deceitful

ceitful prosperity, has left our shores bare, and has opened a waste and desolate prospect of barren sand, and uncultivated country.

I have the honour to be,

My lord, &c.

THE

COMMERCIAL RESTRAINTS

OF

IRELAND

CONSIDERED.

FOURTH LETTER.

THE
COMMERCIAL RESTRAINTS
OF
IRELAND
CONSIDERED.

FOURTH LETTER.

My Lord,
     Dublin, 27th Auguſt, 1779.

THE revenue, for the reaſons already given, decreaſed in 1755†, fell lower in 1756, and ſtill lower in 57. In the laſt year the vaunted proſperity of Ireland was changed into miſery and diſtreſs; the lower claſſes of our people wanted food*; the money ariſing from

---

† Com. Jour. 10 v. 751.
* Ib. 10 v. 16. Speech from the throne, and ib. 25, addreſs from the houſe of commons to the king.

from the extravagance of the rich was freely applied to alleviate the sufferings of the poor‡. One of the first steps of the late duke of Bedford's administration, and which reflects honour on his memory, was obtaining a king's letter, dated 31ft March 1757, for 20,000l to be laid out as his grace should think the most likely to afford the most speedy and effectual relief to his majesty's poor subjects of this kingdom. His grace, in his speech from the throne, humanely expresses his wish, that some method might be found out to prevent the calamities that are the consequences of a want of corn, which had been in part felt the last year, and to which this country had been too often exposed; the commons acknowledge that those calamities had been frequently and were too sensibly and fatally experienced in the course of the last year, thank his grace for his early and charitable attention to the necessities of the poor of this country in their late distresses, and make use of those remarkable expressions, " that " they

† Com. Jour. 10 vol. p. 25, Address from the house of commons to the king.

LET. 4.   OF IRELAND CONSIDERED.   61

" they will moſt chearfully embrace ‡ every
" practicable method to promote tillage †,
They knew that the encouragement of manufactures were the effectual means, and
that thefe means were not in their power.

The ability of the nation was eſtimated by
the money in the treafury, and the penſions
on the civil eſtabliſhment, excluſive of
French, which at Lady-day 1755, were
38,003l. 15s. od. amounted at Lady-day 57,
to 49,293l. 15s. od §.

The fame ideas were entertained of the
refources of this country in the feſſion of
1759. Great Britain had made extraordinary

‡ Com. Jour. 10 vol. 25.
† They brought in a law for the encouragement of tillage, which was ineffectual (fee poſt 42) but the preamble
of that act is a legiſlative proof of the unhappy condition
of the poor of this country before that time. The preamble recites, " the *extreme* neceſſity to which the poor
" of this kingdom had been too frequently reduced for
" want of proviſions."
§ Com. Jour. 10 vol. 285.

nary efforts, and engaged in enormous expences for the protection of the whole empire. This country was in immediate danger of an invasion. Every Irishman was agreed that she should assist Great Britain to the utmost of her ability, but this ability was too highly estimated. The nation abounded rather in loyalty than in wealth †. Our brethren in Great Britain, had, however, formed a different opinion, and surveying their own strength, were incompleat judges of our weakness. A lord lieutenant of too much virtue and magnanimity to speak what he did not think, takes notice from the throne, " of the prosperous state of this " country, improving daily in its manufactures and commerce ‖." His grace had done much to bring it to that state, by obtaining for us some of the best laws * in our books of statutes. But this part of the speech was not taken notice of, either in the address to

† 11 V. 472, Speaker's speech.   ‖ 11 V. 16.
* The acts passed in 58, giving bounties on the landcarriage of corn, and on coals brought to Dublin.

to his majesty, or to his grace, from a house of commons well-disposed to give every mark of duty and respect, and to pay every compliment consistent with truth. The event proved the wisdom of their reserve. The public expences were greatly increased, the pensions on the civil establishment exclusive of French, at Lady-day 1759, amounted to 55,497l. 5s. 0d.* there was at the same time a great augmentation of military expence†. Six new regiments and a troop were raised in a very short space of time. An unanimous and unlimited address of confidence to his grace‡, a specifick vote of credit for 150,000l. ‖, which was afterwards provided for in the loan-bill § of that session, a second vote of credit in the same session for 300,000l. **, the raising the rate of interest paid by government, one per cent, and the payment out of the treasury†† in little more than one year, of 703,957l 3s 1½d ‡‡

were

---

* Com. Jour. 11 Vol. p. 212.   † Ib. from 826, to 837.
‡ Vol. 11, p. 141.   ‖ Ib. 408.   § Ib. 473.
** Ib. 862.   †† Ib,   ‡‡ Ib. 982, from 25th March 59, to 21st of April 60, exclusive.

were the confequences of thofe encreafed expences. The effects of thefe exertions were immediately and feverely felt by the kingdom. Thefe loans could not be fupplied by a poor country, without draining the bankers of their cafh; three of the principal houfes* among them ftopped payment; the three remaining banks in Dublin difcounted no paper, and in fact, did no bufinefs. Public and private credit, that had been drooping fince the year 1754, had now fallen proftrate. At a general meeting of the merchants of Dublin, in April 1760, with feveral members of the houfe of commons, the inability of the former to carry on bufinefs was univerfally acknowledged, not from the want of capital, but from the ftoppage of all paper circulation, and the refufal of the remaining bankers to difcount the bills even of the firft houfes. The merchants and traders of Dublin, in their petition § to the houfe of commons, reprefent

---

* Clements's, Dawfon's and Mitchell's.
§ Com. Jour. 11 Vol. 966. April 15, 1760.

sent " the low state to which public and
" private credit had been of late reduced in
" this kingdom, and particularly in this
" city, of which the successive failures of
" so many banks, and of private traders in
" different parts of this kingdom, in so
" short a time as since October last, were
" incontestable proofs. The petitioners,
" sensible that the necessary consequences
" of these misfortunes must be the loss of
" foreign trade, the diminution of his ma-
" jesty's revenue, and what is still more
" fatal, the decay of the manufactures of
" this kingdom, have in vain repeatedly
" attempted to support the sinking credit
" of the nation by associations and other-
" wise; and are satisfied that no resource
" is now left but what may be expected
" from the wisdom of parliament, to avert
" the calamities with which this kingdom is
" at present threatened."

The committee, to whom it was referred, resolve* that they had proved the several matters

* Com. Jour. 11 Vol. p. 993, 994.

matters alledged in their petition; that the quantity of paper circulating was not near sufficient for supporting the trade and manufactures of this kingdom; and that the house should engage, to the first of May 62, for each of the then subsisting banks in Dublin, to the amount of 50,000l. for each bank; and that an address should be presented to the lord lieutenant, to thank his grace for having given directions that banker's notes should be received as cash from the several subscribers to the loan, and that he would be pleased to give directions that their notes should be taken as cash in all payments at the treasury, and by the several collectors for the city and county of Dublin. The house agreed to those resolutions, and to that for giving credit to the banks, *nem. con.*

The speech from the throne takes notice of the care the house of commons had taken for establishing public credit, which the lord lieutenant says he flatters himself will answer the end proposed, and effect that circulation

LET. 4.   OF IRELAND CONSIDERED.   67

culation so necessary for carrying on the commerce of the country *.

Those facts are not stated as any imputation on the then chief governor: the vigour of his mind incited him to make the crown as useful as possible to the subject, and the subject to the crown. He succeeded in both, but in the latter part of the experiment the weakness of the country was shewn. The great law which we owe to his interposition, I speak of that which gives a bounty on the land carriage of corn and flour to Dublin †, has saved this country from utter destruction; this law, which reflects the highest honour on the author and promoter, is still a proof of the poverty of that country where such a law is necessary. Its true principle is to bring the market of Dublin to the door of the farmer, and that was done in the year ending the 25th of March 1777 at the expence of 61789l. 18s. 6d. to

the

---

* Com. Jour. 11 Vol. p. 1049.
† Brought in by Mr. Pery, the present Speaker.

the public; a large but a most useful and necessary expenditure*. The adoption of this principle proves, what we in this country know to be a certain truth, that there is no other market in Ireland on which the farmer can rely for the certain sale of his corn and flour; a decisive circumstance to shew the wretched state of the manufactures of this kingdom.

In the beginning of the next parliament, the rupture with Spain occasioned a new augmentation of military expence. The ever loyal commons return an address of thanks to the message mentioning the addition of five new battallions †, and unanimously promise to provide for them; and with the same unanimity pass a vote of credit for 200,000l §. The amount of pensions on the civil establishment, exclusive of French,

---

* In the year ending lady-day 1778 it amounted to 71,533l 1s, and in that ending lady-day 1779 to 67,864l. 8s. 10d.
† Com. Jour. 12 Vol. p. 700.   § Ib. 728.

LET. 4.   OF IRELAND CONSIDERED.   69

French, had for one year ending the 25th of March 1761 amounted to 64,127l. 5s.1 and our manufacturers were then diftreffed by the expence and havock of a burthenfome war *.

In the year 1762 a national evil made its appearance, which all the exertions of the government and of the legiflature have not fince been able to eradicate; I mean the rifings of the White Boys. They appear in thofe parts of the kingdom where manufactures are not eftablifhed, and are a proof of the poverty and want of employment of the lower claffes of our people. Lord Northumberland mentions, in his fpeech from the throne † in 1763, that the means of induftry would be the remedy; from whence it feems to follow that the want of thofe means muft be the caufe. To attain this great end the commons promife their attention

‡ Com. Journ. 12 Vol. p. 443.
* Ib. 929, Speech of Lord Hallifax from the throne, 30th April, 1762.
† Ir. Com. Journ. 13 Vol. p. 21.

tion to the proteſtant charter ſchools and linen manufacture‡. The wretched men, who were guilty of thoſe violations of the law, were too mature for the firſt, and totally ignorant of the ſecond; but long eſtabliſhed uſage had given thoſe words a privilege in ſpeeches and addreſſes to ſtand for every thing that related to the improvement of Ireland.

The ſtate of penſions remained nearly the ſame*; by the peace the military expences were conſiderably reduced; of the military eſtabliſhment to be provided for in the ſeſſion 1763, compared with the military eſtabliſhment as it ſtood on the 31ſt of March 1763, the net decreaſe was 119,037l. 0s. 10d. per annum; but as a peace eſtabliſhment it was high, and compared with that of the 31ſt of March 1756 †, being the year preceding

‡ Com. Jour. 13 Vol. p. 23.

* For a year ending 25th March 1763 they were 66,477l. 5s.; they afterwards roſe to 89,095l. 17s. 6d. in September 1777 at the higheſt; and in this year, ending the 25th March laſt, amounted to 85,971l. 2s. 6d.

† Com. Jour. 13 Vol. p. 576.

ceding the laſt war, the annual increaſe was 110,422l. 9s. 5¼d. the debt of the nation at lady-day 1763, and which was entirely incurred in the laſt war, was 521,161l. 16s. 6⅞d.* and would have been much greater if the ſeveral lord lieutenants had not uſed with great œconomy the power of borrowing, which the houſe of commons had from ſeſſion to ſeſſion given them.

That this debt ſhould have been contracted in an expenſive war, in which Ireland was called upon for the firſt time to contribute, is not to be wondered at, but the continual increaſe of this debt, in sixteen years of peace, ſhould be accounted for.

The ſame miſtaken eſtimate of the ability of Ireland, that occaſioned our being called upon to bear part of the Britiſh burthen during the war, produced ſimilar effects at the time of the peace, and after it.

* Com. Jour. 13 Vol. p. 574, 621.

it. The heavy peace eſtabliſhment was increaſed by an augmentation of our army in 1769, which induced an additional charge, taking in the expences of exchange and remittance, of 54,118l. 12s. 6d. yearly, for the firſt year; but this charge was afterwards conſiderably increaſed, and amounted from the year 1769 to Chriſtmas 1778, when it was diſcontinued, to the ſum of 620,824l. 0s. 9½d.; and this increaſed expence was more felt, becauſe it was for the purpoſe of paying forces out of this kingdom.

As our expences increaſed our income diminiſhed; the revenue for the two years, ending the 25th of March 1771 *, was far ſhort of former years, and not nearly ſufficient to pay the charges of government, and the ſums payable for bounties and public works†. The debt of the nation at lady-day 1771, was increaſed to 782,320l. 0s. 0½d‡. The want of income was endeavoured to be ſupplied by a loan. In the money-bill of the October

---

* Com. Jour. 14 Vol. p. 715.   † 15 Vol. p. 710.
‡ Ib. p. 153,

October session 1771, there was a clause impowering government to borrow 200,000l. Immediately after the linen trade declined rapidly; in 1772, 1773, and 1774, the decay in that trade was general in every part of the kingdom where it was established; the quantity manufactured was not above two thirds of what used formerly to be made, and that quantity did not sell for above three-fourths of its former price; the linen and linen yarn exported for one year, ending the 25th of March 1773 ‡, fell short of the exports of one year, ending the 25th of March 1771, to the amount in value of 788,821l. 1s. 3d. At lady-day 1773 *, the debt increased to 994,890l. 10s. 10½d. The attempt in the session of 1773 †, to equalize the annual income and expences failed, and borrowing on tontine in the sessions of 1773, 1775 and 1777, added greatly to the annual expence, and to the sums of money remitted out of the kingdom. The debt now bearing interest

‡ Com. Jour. 16 Vol. p. 372. * Ib. p. 190, 191, 193.
† Ib. 256.

interest amounts to the sum of 1,017,600l. besides a sum of 740,000l. raised on annuities, which amount to 48,900l. yearly, with some incidental expences. The great increase of those national burdens, likely to take place in the approaching session, has been already mentioned.

The debt of Ireland has arisen from the following causes: the expences of the late war, the heavy peace establishment in the year 1763, the increase of that establishment in the year 1769, the sums paid from 1759 to forces out of the kingdom, the great increase of pensions and other additional charges on the civil establishment, which however considerable, bears but a small proportion to the increased military expences, the falling of the revenue, and the sums paid for bounties and public works; these are mentioned last, because it is apprehended that they have not operated to increase this debt in so great a degree as some persons have imagined; for though the amount is large, yet no part of the money

was

was sent out of the kingdom, and several of the grants were for useful purposes, some of which made returns to the public and to the treasury exceeding the amount of those grants.

When those facts are considered, no doubt can be entertained but that the supposed wealth of Ireland has led to real poverty; and when it is known, that from the year 1751 to Christmas 1778 the sums, remitted by Ireland to pay troops serving abroad, amounted to the sum of 1,401,925l. 19s. 4d. it will be equally clear from whence this poverty has principally arisen.

In those seasons of expence and borrowing, the lower classes were equally subject to poverty and distress, as in the periods of national œconomy. In 1762 lord Hallifax, in his speech from the throne*, acknowledges that our manufactures were distressed by the war. In 1763, the corporation

Com. Jour. 12 Vol. p. 928.

tion of weavers, by a petition to the houfe of commons, complain that, notwithftanding the great increafe both in number and wealth of the inhabitants of the metropolis, they found a very great decay of feveral very valuable branches of trade and manufactures * of this city, particularly in the filken and woollen.

In 1765 there was a fcarcity caufed by the failure of potatoes in general throughout the kingdom, which diftreffed the common people; the fpring corn had alfo failed, and grain was fo high, that it was thought neceffary to appoint a committee † to inquire what may be the beft method to reduce it; and to prevent a great dearth, two acts were paffed early in that feffion, to ftop the diftillery, and to prevent the exportation of corn, for a limitted time. In fpring 1766 thofe fears appeared to have been well-founded; feveral towns were in great diftrefs for corn; and by the humanity of the lord

---

* Com. Jour. 13 Vol. p. 987.
† Ib. 14 Vol. p. 69, 114, 151.

lord lieutenant, lord Hertford, money was issued out of the treasury to buy corn for such places as applied to his lordship for that relief.

The years 1770 and 1771 were seasons of great distress in Ireland, and in the month of February in the latter year, the high price of corn is mentioned from the throne*, as an object of the first importance, which demanded the utmost attention.

In 1778 and 1779 there was great plenty of corn, but the manufacturers were not able to buy, and many thousands of them were supported by charity; the consequence was that corn fell to so low a price that the farmers in many places were unable to pay their rents, and every where were under great difficulties.

That the linen manufacture has been of the utmost consequence to this country, that

* Com. Jour. 14 Vol. p. 665.

that it has greatly profpered, that it has been long encouraged by the protection of Great Britain, that whatever wealth Ireland is poffeffed of arifes, for the moft part, from that trade, is freely acknowledged; but in far the greateft part of the kingdom it has not yet been eftablifhed, and many attempts to introduce it have, after long perfeverance and great expence, proved fruitlefs.

Though that manufacture made great advances from 1727 to 1758*, yet the tillage of this kingdom declined during the whole of that period, and we have not fince been free from fcarcity.

Notwithftanding the fuccefs of that manufacture, the bulk of our people have always continued poor, and in a great many feafons have wanted food. Can the hiftory of any other fruitful country on the globe, enjoying peace for fourfcore years, and not vifited by plague or peftilence, produce fo many

* Com. Jour. 16 Vol. p. 467, report from committee, nd ib. 501 agreed to by the houfe, *nem. con.*

many recorded inftances of the poverty and wretchednefs, and of the reiterated want and mifery of the lower orders of the people? There is no fuch example in ancient or modern ftory. If the ineffectual endeavours by the reprefentatives of thofe poor people to give them employment and food, had not left fufficient memorials of their wretchednefs; if their habitations, apparel, and food were not fufficient proofs, I fhould appeal to the human countenance for my voucher, and reft the evidence on that hopelefs defpondency that hangs on the brow of unemployed induftry.

That fince the fuccefs of the linen manufacture, the money and the rents of Ireland have been greatly increafed, is acknowledged; but it is affirmed, and the fact is of notoriety, that the lower orders, not of that trade, are not lefs wretched. Thofe employed in the favoured manufacture generally buy from that country to which they principally fell; and the rife in lands is a misfortune to the poor, where their wages

do

do not rife proportionably, which will not happen where manufactures and agriculture are not sufficiently encouraged. Give premiums by land or by water, arrange your exports and imports in what manner you will; if you difcourage the people from working up the principal materials of their country, the bulk of that people muft ever continue miferable, the growth of the nation will be checked, and the finews of the ftate enfeebled.

I have ftated a tedious detail of inftances, to fhew that the fufferings of the lower claffes of our people have continued the fame (with an exception only of thofe employed in the linen trade) fince the time of queen Anne, as they were during her reign; that the caufe remains the fame, namely, that our manufacturers have not fufficient employment, and cannot afford to buy from the farmer, and that therefore manufactures and agriculture muft both be prejudiced.

After

LET. 4. OF IRELAND CONSIDERED. 81

After revolving thofe repeated inftances, and almoft continued chain of diftrefs, for fuch a feries of years, among the inhabitants of a temperate climate, furrounded by the bounties of providence and the means of abundance, and being unable to difcover any accidental or natural caufes for thofe evils, we are led to inquire whether they have arifen from the miftaken policy of man.

I have the honour to be,

My lord, &c.

THE
COMMERCIAL RESTRAINTS
OF
IRELAND
CONSIDERED.

FIFTH LETTER.

THE COMMERCIAL RESTRAINTS OF IRELAND CONSIDERED.

FIFTH LETTER.

My Lord,

Dublin, 30th Aug. 1779.

EVERY man of discernment, who attends to the facts which have been stated, would conclude, that there must be some political institutions in this country counteracting the natural course of things, and obstructing the prosperity of the people. Those institutions should be considered, that as from the effects the cause has been traced, this also should be examined, to shew that such consequences are necessarily deducible from it. For several years the

the exportation of live cattle to England* was the principal trade of Ireland. This was thought most erroneously, ‡ as has since been acknowledged §, to lower the rents of lands in England. From this and perhaps from some less worthy motive ** a law passed in England ††, to restrain and afterwards to prohibit the exportation of cattle from Ireland. The Irish deprived of their principal trade, and reduced to the utmost distress by this prohibition, had no resource but to work up their own commodities, to which they applied themselves with great ardor ‡‡. After this prohibition they increased their number of sheep, and at the revolution were possessed of very numerous flocks. They had good

* Carte, 2 vol. 318, 319.
‡ Sir W. Petty's Political Survey, 69, 70. Sir W. Temple, 3 vol. 22, 23.
§ By several British acts (32 C. 2, ch. 11. 5 G. 3, ch. 10. 12 G. 3, ch. 56.) allowing from time to time the free importation of all sorts of cattle from Ireland.
** Personal prejudice against the duke of Ormond. (2 Carte, 332, 337.
†† 15 Ch. 2, ch. 7. 18 Ch. 2, ch. 2.
‡‡ 2 Carte, 332.

good reasons to think that this object of industry was not only left open, but recommended to them. The ineffectual attempt by lord Strafford in 1639, to prevent the making of broad cloths in Ireland*, the relinquishment of that scheme by never afterwards reviving it, the encouragement given to their woollen manufactures by many English acts of parliament from the reign of Edward the 3d † to the 12th of Ch. 2d, and several of them for the express purpose of exportation; the letter of Charles the 2d, in 1667, with the advice of his privy council in England, and the proclamation in pursuance of that letter, encouraging the exportation of their manufactures to foreign countries; by the Irish statutes of the 13th Hen. 8, ch. 2, 28th Hen. 8, ch. 17, of the 11th Elizabeth, Ch. 10, and 17 and 18 Ch. 2, ch. 15, (all of which, the act of 28 Henry 8th excepted, received the approbation of the privy council of England, having been returned

---

* Com. Jour. 1 vol. p. 208, by a clause to be inserted in an Irish act.

† See post, those acts stated.

turned under the great seal of that kingdom) afforded as strong grounds of assurance as any country could possess for the continuance of any trade or manufacture.

Great numbers of their flocks had been destroyed at the time of the revolution, but they were replaced at great expence, and became more numerous and flourishing than before. The woollen manufacture was cultivated in Ireland for ages before, and for several years after the revolution, without any appearance of jealousy from England, the attempt by lord Strafford excepted. No discouragement is intimated in any speech from the throne until the year 1698. lord Sydney's in 1692 imparts the contrary, " their " majesties, says he*, being in their own roy- " al judgments satisfied that a country so " fertile by nature, and so advantageously " situated for *trade and navigation*, can want " nothing but the blessing of peace, and the " help of some good laws to make it as rich " and flourishing *as most of its neighbours*; I am " ordered to assure you, that nothing shall
" be

* Com. Jour 2 Vol. p. 576.

LET. 5.   OF IRELAND CONSIDERED.   89

" be wanting on their parts that may con-
" tribute to your perfect and lasting hap-
" piness."

Several laws had been made * in England to prevent the exportation of wool, yarn made of wool, fuller's earth, or any kind of scowering earth or fulling clay from England or Ireland, into any places out of the kingdoms of England or Ireland. But those laws were equally restrictive on both kingdoms.

In the first year† of William and Mary certain ports were mentioned in Ireland, from which only wool should be shipped from that kingdom, and certain ports in England into which only it should be imported; and a register was directed to be kept in the custom-house of London of all the wool, from time to time, imported from Ireland. By a subsequent act in this reign‡, passed in 1696, the commissioners or farmers of the customs

in

* English acts, 12 Ch. 2 ch. 32. 13 and 14 Ch. 2 ch. 18
1 W. and M. Ch. 32.   † 7 and 8 W. ch. 28.

in Ireland are directed, once in every six months, to transmit to the commissioners of customs in England, an account of all wool exported from Ireland to England, and this last act, in its title, professes the intention of encouraging the importation of wool from Ireland. The prohibition of exporting the materials from either kingdom, except to the other, and the encouragement to export it from Ireland to England, mentioned in the title of the last-mentioned act, but for which no provision seems to be made, unless the designation of particular ports may be so called, was the system that then seemed to be settled, for preventing the wool of Ireland from being prejudicial to England; but the prevention of the exportation of the manufacture was an idea that seemed never to have been entertained until the year 1697, when a bill for that purpose was brought into the English house of commons*, and passed that house; but after great consideration was not passed by the lords in that parliament.

14th Jan. 1697.

parliament †. There does not appear to have been any increase at that time in the woollen manufacture of Ireland, sufficient to have raised any jealousy in England.

By a report from the commissioners of trade in that kingdom, dated on the 23d December 97, and laid before the house of commons, in 1698 they find that the woollen manufacture in Ireland had increased since the year 1665, as follows:

Years.	New draperies Pieces.	Old draperies. Pieces.	Frize Yards.
1665	224	32	444,381
1687	11,360	103	1,129,716
1696	4,413	$34\frac{1}{2}$	104,167

The bill for restraining the exportation of woollen manufactures from Ireland was brought into the English house of commons on the 23d of Feb. 97, but the law did not pass until the year 1699, in the first session of the new parliament. I have not been able

† 7 July 1698 dissolved

able to obtain an account of the exportation of woollen manufactures for the year 1697†, but from the 25th of December 1697, to the 25th of December 1698, being the first year in which the exports in books extant, are registered in the custom-house at Dublin, the amount appears to be of

New drapery. Pieces.	Old drapery. Pieces.	Frize. Yds.
23,285½	281½	666,901

though this encreafe of export fhews that the trade was advancing in Ireland, yet the total amount or the comparative increafe since

---

† In a pamphlet cited by Dr. Smith, (v. 2, p. 244.) in his memoirs, of wool it is faid that the total value of thofe manufactures exported in 1697, was 23,614l 9s 6d namely, in frizes and stockings 14,625l 12s; in old and new draperies 8988l 17s 6d, and that though the Irifh had been every year increafing yet they had not recovered above one third of the woollen trade which they had before the war (ib. 243). The value in 1687, according to the fame authority, was 70,521l 14s, of which the frizes were 56,485l 16s. Stockings 2520l. 18s, and old and new drapery (which it is there faid could alone interfere with the Englifh trade) 11,514l 10s.

since 1687 could scarcely "sink the value of "lands, and tend to the ruin of the trade "and woollen manufactures of England §."

The apprehensions of England seem rather to have arisen from the fears of future, than from the experience of any past rivalship in this trade. I have more than once heard lord Bowes, the late chancellor of this kingdom, mention a conversation that he had with sir Robert Walpole on this subject, who assured him that the jealousies entertained in England, of the woollen trade in Ireland, and the restraints of that trade had at first taken their rise from the boasts of some of our countrymen in London, of the great success of that manufacture here. Whatever was the cause, both houses of parliament in England addressed king William, in very strong terms, on this subject; but on considering those addresses they seem to be founded, not on the state at that time of that manufacture here, but the probability
of

§ Preamble of English act of 1699.

of its further increase. As those proceedings are of great importance to two of the principal manufactures of this country, it is thought necessary to state them particularly. The lords represent, "that the *growing* manufacture of cloth in Ireland‡, both by the cheapness of all sorts of necessaries for life, and *goodness of materials for making all manner of cloth*, doth invite your subjects of England with their families and servants to leave their habitations to settle there, to the increase of the woollen manufacture in Ireland, which makes your loyal subjects in this kingdom very apprehensive that *the further growth* of it *may* greatly prejudice the said manufacture here; by which the trade of the nation and the value of lands will very much decrease, and the numbers of your people be much lessened here;" they then beseech his majesty "in the most public and effectual way, that may be, to declare to all your subjects of Ireland, that the *growth* and

‡ 9th June 1698, vol. of lords journals, page 314.

" and *increase* of the woollen manufacture
" hath long, and will ever be looked upon
" with jealousy, by all your subjects of this
" kingdom; *and if not timely remedied* may
" occasion very strict laws, totally to prohi-
" bit and suppress the same; and on the
" other hand if they turn their industry and
" skill, to the settling and improving the
" linen manufacture, for which generally
" the lands of that kingdom are very pro-
" per, they shall receive all countenance, fa-
" vour and protection from your *royal influ-*
" *ence*, for the encouragement and promo-
" ting of the said linen manufacture, to *all*
" *the advantage and profit that kingdom can be*
" *capable of.*"

King William in his answer says, "his majesty will take care to do what their lordships have desired;" and the lords direct that the lord chancellor should order that the address and answer be forthwith printed and published §.

In

§ Lord's Jour. page 315.

In the addrefs of the commons § they say, that "being fenfible that the wealth and "peace of this kingdom do, in a great mea- "fure, depend on preferving the woollen "manufacture, as much as poffible, *entire* "to this realm, they think it becomes them, "like their anceftors, to be jealous of the "*eftablifhment* and *increafe* thereof elfewhere; "and to ufe their utmoft endeavours to pre- "vent it, and therefore, they cannot with- "out trouble obferve, that Ireland, depen- "dant on, and protected by England in the "enjoyment of all they have, and which is "fo proper for the linen manufacture, the "eftablifhment and growth of which there "would be fo enriching to themfelves, and "fo profitable to England, fhould *of late* "apply itfelf to the woollen manufacture, "to the great prejudice of the trade of this "kingdom, and fo unwillingly promote the "linen trade, which would benefit both "them and us.

The

§ 30th June 1698.

- "The confequence whereof will neceffitate
"your parliament of England to interpofe, to
"prevent the mifchief that *threatens* us, un-
"lefs your majefty, by your authority and
"great wifdom, fhall find means to fecure
"the trade of England by making your fub-
"jects of Ireland to purfue the joint inte-
"reft of both kingdoms."

"And we do moft humbly implore your
"majefty's protection and favour in this
"matter; and that you will make it your
"royal care, and enjoin all thofe you em-
"ploy in Ireland, to make it their care, and
"ufe their utmoft diligence, to hinder the
"*exportation of wool* from Ireland, except to
"be imported hither, and for the difcourag-
"ing the woollen manufactures, and encou-
"raging the linen manufactures in Ireland,
"to which we fhall be *always* ready to give
"our *utmoft* affiftance."

This addrefs was prefented to his majefty by the houfe. The anfwer is explicit. " I
" fhall do all that in me lies to difcourage
"the

"the woollen trade in Ireland, and encou-
"rage the linen manufacture there; and
"to promote the trade of England."

He soon after wrote a letter § to lord Galway, then one of the lords justices of this kingdom, in which he tells him, "that it
"was never of such importance to have at
"present a good session of parliament, not
"only in regard to my affairs of that king-
"dom, but especially of this here. The chief
"thing that must be tried to be prevented is,
"that the Irish parliament takes no notice of
"what has passed in this here †, and that you
"make effectual laws for the linen manufac
"ture, and discourage *as far as possible* the
"woollen." It would be unjust to infer from any of those proceedings that this great prince wanted affection for this country. They were times of party. He was often under the necessity of complying against his own opinion and wishes, and about this time was obliged to send away his favourite

§ 16th July 1698.   † Rapin's Hist. v. 17, p. 417.

LET. 5. OF IRELAND CONSIDERED. 99

favourite guards, in compliance with the defire of the commons.

The houfes of parliament in England originally intended, that the bufinefs fhould be done in the parliament of Ireland by the exertion of that great and juft influence which king William had acquired in that kingdom. On the firft day of the following feffion § the lords juftices, in their fpeech, mention a bill tranfmitted for the encouragement of the linen and hempen manufactures, which they recommend in the following words, " the fettlement of this " manufacture will contribute much to peo- " ple the country, and will be found *much* " *more advantageous to this kingd m* than the " woollen manufacture, which being the " fettled ftaple trade of England, *from* " *whence all foreign markets* are fupplied, can " never be encouraged *here* for that purpofe ; " whereas the linen and hempen manufac- " tures will not only be encouraged, as con-
" fiftent

§ 27th September 1698, vol. 2. p. 994.

"siftent with the trade of England, but will
"render the trade of this kingdom both use-
"ful and neceffary to England."

The commons in their addrefs § promife their hearty endeavours to eftablifh a linen and hempen manufacture in Ireland, and fay that they hoped to find fuch a temperament in refpect to the woollen trade here, that the fame may not be injurious to England. They referred the confideration of that fubject to the committee of fupply, who refolved that an additional duty be laid on old and new drapery of the manufacture of this kingdom † that fhall be exported, frizes excepted; to which the houfe agreed *. But there were petitions prefented againft this duty, and relative to the quantity of it, and the committee appointed to confider of this duty were not it feems fo expeditious in their proceedings as the impatience of the times required ‡.

On

§ Com. Jour. 2 Vol. p. 997.   † Ib. 2 vol. p. 1022.
* October 24, 1698.
‡ Com. Jour. v. 2, p. 1007, 1035.

On the 2d of October the lords juftices made a quickening fpeech to both houfes, taking notice, that the progrefs which they expected was not made, in the bufinefs of the feffion, and ufe thofe remarkable words, " The matters we recommended to you are fo " neceffary, and the profperity of this king- " dom depends fo much on the good fuccefs " of this feffion, that fince we know his " majefty's affairs cannot permit your fitting " very long, we thought the greateft mark " we could give of our kindnefs and con- " cern for you, was to come hither, and " defire you to haften the difpatch of the " matters under your confideration; in " which we are the more earneft, becaufe " we muft be fenfible, that if the prefent " opportunity his majefty's affection to you " hath put into your hands be loft, it feems " hardly to be recovered ‡."

On the 2d of January 1698, O. S. the houfe refolved, that the report from the committee of the whole houfe, appointed to confider

‡ Com. Jour. p. 1032.

confider of a duty to be laid on the woollen manufactures of this kingdom, fhould be made on the next day, and nothing to intervene. But on that day a meffage was delivered from the lords juftices in the following words, " We have received his ma-
" jeftys commands† to fend unto you a bill,
" entitled an act for laying an additional
" duty upon woollen manufactures exported
" out of this kingdom; the paffing of which
" in this feffion his majefty recommends to
" you, as what may be of great advantage
" for the prefervation of the trade of this
" kingdom."

The bill which accompanied this meffage was prefented, and a queftion for receiving it was carried in the affirmative, by 74 againft 34. This bill muft have been tranfmited from the council of Ireland. Whilft the commons were proceeding with the utmoft temper and moderation, were exerting great firmnefs in reftraining all attempts to enflame

the

† Com. Jour. 2 Vol. p. 1082.

the minds of the people †, and were deliberating on the moſt important ſubject that could ariſe, it was taken out of their hands‡; but the bill paſſed though not without oppoſition*, and received the royal aſſent on the 29th day of January 1698.

By this act an additional duty was impoſed of 4s. for every 20s. in value of broad cloth exported out of Ireland, and 2s. on every 20s. in value of new drapery, frizes only excepted, from the 25th of March 99, to the 25th March, 1702 ‖; the only woollen manufacture excepted was one of which Ireland had been in poſſeſſion before the reign of Edward the 3d, and in which ſhe had been always diſtinguiſhed ‡. This law has every appearance of having being framed on the part of adminiſtration.

But

Com. Jour. 2 vol. 1007. * Com. Jour. 1104, by 105, againſt 41. ‖ 10 W. 3 ch. 5.

‡ And. on Com. Vol. 1. 204.

§ The commiſſioners of trade in England by their repreſentation of the 11th October 1698, ſay, (Eng. Com. Jour. 12 vol. 437.) "they conceive it not neceſſary to make any alteration whatſoever in this act," but take notice that the duties on broad cloth, of which very little is made in Ireland, is 20 per cent; but the duty on new drapery, of which much is made, is but 10 per cent.

but it did not satisfy the English parliament, where a perpetual law was made, prohibiting, from the 20th of June, 1699*, the exportation from Ireland of all goods made or mixed with wool, except to England and Wales, and with the licenſe of the commiſſioners of the revenue; duties † had been before laid on the importation into England equal to a prohibition, therefore this act has operated as a total prohibition of the exportation.

Before theſe laws the Iriſh were under great diſadvantages in the woollen trade, by not being allowed to export their woollen manufactures to the Engliſh colonies §, or to import dye ſtuffs directly from thence; and the Engliſh in this reſpect, and in havin thoſe excluſive markets, poſſeſſed conſiderable advantages.

Let it now be conſidered what are the uſual means taken to promote the proſperity

---

* Eng. Stat. 10 and 11 Wil. III. ch. 10, paſſed in 1699. † 12 Ch. II. ch. 4, Eng. and afterwards continued by 11 Geo. I. ch. 7. Brit.

§ By an Eng. act, made in 1663, the ſame which laid the firſt reſtraint on the exportation of cattle.

rity of any country in refpect of trade and manufactures. She is encouraged to work up her own materials, to export her manufactures to other nations, to import from them the materials for manufacture, and to export none of her own that fhe is able to work up, not to buy what fhe is capable of felling to others, and to promote the carrying trade and fhip-building. If thefe are the moft obvious means by which a nation may advance in ftrength and riches, inftitutions counteracting thofe means muft neceffarily tend to reduce it to weaknefs and poverty; and therefore the advocates for the continuance of thofe inftitutions will find it difficult to fatisfy the world that fuch a fyftem of policy is either reafonable or juft.

The cheapnefs of labour, the excellence of materials, and the fuccefs of the manufacture in the excluded country*, may appear to an unprejudiced man to be rather reafons

---

* See the Addrefs of the Englifh Houfe of Lords.

sons for the encouragement than for the prohibition. But the preamble of the English act of the 10th and 11th of William III. affirms, that the exportation from Ireland and the English plantations in America to foreign markets, heretofore supplied from England, would inevitably sink the value of lands, and tend to the ruin of the trade and manufactures of that realm. I shall only consider this assertion as relative to Ireland. A fact upon which the happiness of a great and ancient kingdom, and of millions of people depends, ought to have been supported by the most incontestible evidence, and should never be suffered to rest in speculation, or to be taken from the mere suggestion or distant apprehension of commercial jealousy. Those fears for the future were not founded on any experience of the past. From what market had the woollen manufactures of Ireland ever excluded England? What part of her trade, and which of her manufactures had been ruined, and where did any of her lands fall by the woollen exports of Ireland? Were

any

any of thofe facts attempted to be proved at the time of the prohibition? The amount of the Irish export proves it to have been impoffible that thofe facts could have then exifted. The confequences mentioned as likely to arife to England from the fuppofed increafe of thofe manufactures in Ireland, had no other foundation but the apprehenfions of rivalfhip among trading people, who, in excluding their fellow-citizens, have opened the gates for the admiffion of the enemy.

Whether thofe apprehenfions are now well founded, fhould be carefully confidered. Juftice, found policy, and the general good of the Britifh empire require it. The arguments in fupport of thofe reftraints are principally thefe:—That labour is cheaper and taxes lower in Ireland than in England, and that the former would be able to underfell the latter in all foreign markets.

Spinning is now certainly cheaper in Ireland, becaufe the perfons employed in it
live

live on food* with which the English would not be content; but the wages of spinners would soon rise if the trade was opened. At the loom, I am informed, that the same quantity of work is done cheaper in England than in Ireland; and we have the misfortune of daily experience to convince us that the English, notwithstanding the supposed advantages of the Irish in this trade, undersell them at their own markets in every branch of the woollen manufacture. A decisive proof that they cannot undersell the English in foreign markets.

With the increase of manufactures, agriculture and commerce in Ireland, the demand for labour, and consequently its price, would increase §. That price would be soon higher in Ireland than in England. It is not in the richest countries, but in those that are growing rich the fastest, that the wages of labour are highest †, though the price of

---

* Potatoes and milk, or more frequently water.
§ Dr. Smith's Wealth of Nations, 1 vol. p. 94.
† Ib. 85, 86.

of provisions is much lower in the latter; this, before the present rebellion, was in both respects the case of England and North America. Any difference in the price of labour is more than balanced by the difference in the price of the material, which has been for many years past higher in Ireland than in England, and would become more valuable if the export of the manufacture was allowed. The English have also great advantages in this trade from their habits of diligence, superior skill and large capitals. From these circumstances, though the Scotch have full liberty to export their woollen manufactures, the English work up their wool*, and the Scotch make only some kinds of coarse cloaths for the lower classes of their people; and this is said to be for want of a capital to manufacture it at home §. If the woollen trade was now open to Ireland, it would be for the most part

---

* Dr. Smith's Wealth of Nations, 1 Vol. p. 445. Dr. Campbell's Polit. Survey of Great Britain, 2 Vol. p. 159. Anderson on Industry.

§ Smith, ib.

part carried on by English capitals, and by merchants resident there. Nearly one half of the stock which carried on the foreign trade of Ireland in 1672, inconsiderable as it then was, belonged to those who lived out of Ireland *. The greater part of the exportation and coasting trade of British America was carried on by the capitals of merchants who resided in Great Britain; even many of the stores and ware-houses from which goods were retailed in some of their principal provinces, particularly in Virginia and Maryland, belonged to merchants who resided in Great Britain, and the retail trade was carried on by those who were not resident in the country †. It is said that in ancient Egypt, China and Indostan, the greater part of their exportation trade was carried on by foreigners §. The same thing happened formerly in Ireland, where the whole commerce of the country was carried on by the Dutch ‡; and at present in the victualling

---

* Sir Wil Petty's Polit. Survey of Ireland, p. 90.
† Smith's Wealth of Nations, 1 Vol. p. 446. § Ib.
‡ Lord Strafford's Letters, 1 Vol. p. 33.

LET. 5.   OF IRELAND CONSIDERED.   111

victualling trade of Ireland, the Irish are but factors to the English. This is not without example in Great Britain, where there are many little manufacturing towns, the inhabitants of which have not capitals sufficient to transport the produce of their own industry to those distant markets where there is demand and consumption for it, and their merchants are properly only the agents of wealthier merchants, who reside in some of the greater commercial cities †. The Irish are deficient in all kinds of stock, they have not sufficient for the cultivation of their lands, and are deficient in the stocks of master manufacturers, wholesale merchants, and even of retailers.

Of what Ireland gains it is computed that one third centers in Great Britain §. Of our woollen manufacture the greatest part of the profit would go directly there. But the manufacturers of Ireland would be employed, would

† Smith's Wealth of Nations, 1 Vol. p. 445.
§ Sir M. Decker's decline of foreign trade, p. 155, and Anderson on Commerce, 2 Vol. p. 149.

would be enabled to buy from the farmers the superfluous produce of their labour, the people would become industrious, their numbers would greatly increase, the British state would be strengthened, though probably this country would not for many years find any great influx of wealth; it would be however more equally distributed, from which the people and the government would derive many important advantages.

Whatever wealth might be gained by Ireland would be, in every respect, an accession to Great Britain. Not only a considerable part of it would flow to the seat of government, and of final judicature, and to the centre of commerce; but when Ireland should be able she would be found willing, as in justice she ought to be, to bear her part of those expences which Great Britain may hereafter incur, in her efforts for the protection of the whole British empire. If Ireland chearfully and spontaneously, but when she was ill able, contributed, particularly in the years 1759, 1761 and 1769, and continued to do so in the midst of distress and poverty, without murmur, to the end of the year 1778, when Great Britain thought proper to relieve her from a burden which she was no longer able to bear, no doubt can be entertained of her contributing, in a much greater proportion, when the means of acquiring shall be opened to her.

I form this opinion, not only from the proofs which the experience of many years, and in many signal instances has given, but the nature of the Irish constitution, which requires that the laws of Ireland should be certified under the great seal of England, and the superintending protection of Great Britain, necessary to the existence of Ireland, would make it her interest to cultivate, at all times, a good understanding with her sister kingdom.

The lowness of taxes in Ireland seems to fall within the objection arising from the cheapness of labour. But the disproportion between the taxes of the two kingdoms is much overrated in Great Britain. Hearth-money in Ireland amounts to about 59,000l. yearly, the fums raifed by Grand Juries are faid to exceed the annual fum of 140,000l. and the duties on beef, butter, pork and tallow exported, at a medium from 1772 to 1778, amount to 26,577l. 11s. yearly. Thefe are payable out of lands, or their immediate produce, and may well be confidered as a land tax. Thefe with the many other taxes payable in Ireland, compared either with the annual amount of the fums which the inhabitants can earn or expend, with the rentall of the lands, the amount of the circulating fpecie, of perfonal property, or of the trade of Ireland, it is apprehended would appear not to be inferior in proportion to the taxes of England, compared with any of thofe objects in that country†. The fums remitted to abfentees*, are worfe than fo much

---

† Compare the circumftances of the two countries in one of thofe articles, which affects all the reft. The fums raifed in Great Britain in time of peace are faid to amount to ten millions, in Ireland to more than one million yearly. The circulating cafh of the former is eftimated at 23 millions, of the latter at two.

See poft. 59.

much paid in taxes, becaufe a large proportion of thefe is ufually expended in the country. If this reafoning is admitted, it will require no calculation to fhew that Ireland pays more taxes in proportion to its fmall income, than England does in proportion to its great one.

Of excifable commodities, the confumption by each manufacturer is not fo confiderable as to make the great difference commonly imagined in the price of labour. It is an acknowledged fact that Ireland pays in excifes as much as fhe is able to bear, and that her inability to bear more arifes from thofe very reftraints. But fuppofing the difproportion to be as great as is erroneoufly imagined in Great Britain, it will not conclude in favour of the prohibition. The land-tax is nearly four times as high in fome counties of England as in others, and provifions are much cheaper in fome parts of that kingdom than in others, and yet they have all fufficient employment, and go to market upon equal terms. But a

monopoly

monopoly and not an equal market was plainly the object in 1698; it was not to prevent the Irish from underselling at foreign markets, but to prevent their selling there at all. The consequences to the excluded country have been mentioned. England has also been a great sufferer by this mistaken policy.

Mr. Dobbs, who wrote in 1729*, affirms that by this law of 1699, our wollen manufacturers were forced away into France, Germany and Spain; that they had in many branches so much improved the woollen manufacture of France, as not only to supply themselves, but to vie with the English in foreign markets, and that by their correspondence, they had laid the foundation for the running of wool thither both from England and Ireland. He says that those nations were then so improved, as in a great measure to supply themselves with many sorts they formerly had from England, and since that time have deprived Britain

* Essay on the Trade of Ireland, p. 6, 7.

Britain of millions, inſtead of the thouſands that Ireland might have made.

It is now acknowledged that the French underſell the Engliſh; and as far as they are ſupplied with Iriſh wool, the loſs to the Britiſh empire is double what it would be, if the Iriſh exported their goods manufactured. This is mentioned by Sir Matthew Decker*, as the cauſe of the decline of the Engliſh, and the increaſe of the French woollen manufactures; and he aſſerts that the Iriſh can recover that trade out of their hands. England, ſince the paſſing this law, has got much leſs of our wool than before †. In 1698, the export of our wool to England amounted to 377,520¾ ſtone; at a medium of eight years, to lady-day 1728, it was only 227,049 ſtone, which is 148,000 ſtone leſs than in 1698, and was a loſs of more than half a million yearly to England. In the laſt ten years the quantity exported has been ſo greatly reduced, that in one of theſe years ‡ it amounted

---

* Decline of foreign trade, p. 55, 56, 155.
† Dobbs, p. 76.   ‡ In 1774.

mounted only to 1007 ft. 11 lb. and in the laſt year did not exceed 1665 ft. 12 lb. *. The price of wool, under an abſolute prohibition, is 50l. or 60l. per cent. under the market price of Europe, which will always defeat the prohibition †.

The impracticability of preventing the pernicious practice of running wool is now well underſtood. Of the thirty-two counties in Ireland nineteen are maritime, and the reſt are waſhed by a number of fine rivers that empty themſelves into the ſea. Can ſuch an extent of ocean, ſuch a range of coaſts, ſuch a multitude of harbours, bays and creeks be effectually guarded?

The prohibition of the export of live cattle forced the Iriſh into the re-eſtabliſhment

---

* Nor was this deficiency made up by the exportation of yarn. The quantities of theſe ſeveral articles exported from 1764 to 1778, are mentioned in the Appendix, Numb.

† Smith's Memoirs of Wool, 2 Vol. p. 554. The only way to prevent it, is to enable us to work it up at home. Ib. 293.

ment of their woollen manufacture; and the reſtraint of the woollen manufacture was a ſtrong temptation to the running of wool. The ſevereſt penalties were enacted, the Britiſh legiſlature, the government and houſe of commons of Ireland, exerted all poſſible efforts to remove this growing evil, but in vain, until the law was made in Great Britain * in 1739, to take off the duties from woollen or bay yarn exported from Ireland, excepting worſted yarn of two or more threads, which has certainly given a conſiderable check to the running of wool, and has ſhewn that the policy of opening is far more efficacious than that of reſtraining. The world is become a great commercial ſociety, exclude trade from one channel, and it ſeldom fails to find another.

To ſhew the abſolute neceſſity of Great Britain's opening to Ireland ſome new means of acquiring, let the annual balance of exports and

* This was done for the benefit of the woollen manufacture in England. Eng. Com. Jour. 22 Vol. p. 442.

and imports, returned from the entries in the different cuftom houfes, in favour of Ireland, on all her trade with the whole world, in every year from 1768 to 1778, be compared with the remittances made from Ireland to England in each of thofe years, it will evidently appear that thofe remittances could not be made out of that balance. The entries of exports made at cuftom houfes are well known to exceed the real amount of thofe exports in all countries, and this excefs is greater in times of diffidence, when merchants wifh to acquire credit by giving themfelves the appearance of being great traders.

This balance in favour of Ireland on her general trade, appears by thofe returns to have been in 1776, 606,190l. 11s. 0½d. in 1777, 24,203l. 3s. 10½d. in 1778, 386,384l. 5s. 7d. and taken at a medium of eleven years from 1768 to 1778, both inclufive, it amounts to the fum of 605,083l. 7s. 5d. The fums remitted from Ireland to Great-Britain for rents, intereft of of money, penfions, falaries and profits of offices amounted, at the loweft computation, from 1768 to 1773, to 1,100,000l. yearly *; and from 1773, when the tontines were introduced, from which period large fums were borrowed from England, thofe remittances were confiderably increafed, and are now not lefs than between 12 and 13000l. yearly. Ireland then pays to Great-Britain double the fum that fhe collects from the whole world in all the trade which Great-Britain allows her. It will be difficult to find a fimilar inftance in the hiftory of mankind.

Thofe great and conftant iffues of her wealth without any return, not felt by any other country in fuch a degree, are reafons for granting advantages to Ireland to fupply this confuming wafte, inftead of depriving her of any which Nature has beftowed.

* This is ftated confiderably under the computation made in the lift of abfentees publifhed in Dublin in 1769, which makes the amount at that time 1,208,982l. 14s. 6d.

If any of the refources, which have hitherto enabled her to bear this prodigious drain, are injurious to the manufactures both of England and Ireland, and highly advantageous to the rivals and enemies of both, is it wife in Great-Britain by perfevering in an impracticable fyftem of commercial policy, repugnant to the natural courfe and order of things, to fuffer fo very confiderable a part of the empire to remain in fuch a fituation?

The experiment of an equal and reafonable fyftem of commerce is worth making; that which has been found the beft conductor in philofophy is the fureft guide in commerce.

Would you confult perfons employed in the trade? They have in one refpect an intereft oppofite to that of the public. To narrow the competition is advantageous to the dealers*, but prejudicial to the public. If Edward the firft had not preferred the general

---

* Smith's Wealth of Nations, 1 Vol. 316.

general welfare of his subjects to the interested opinions and petitions of the traders, all merchant traders (who were then mostly strangers) would have been sent away from London †, for which purpose the commons offered him the 50th part of their moveables*.

What was the information given by the trading towns in 1697 and 1698, on the subject of the woollen manufacture of Ireland, several of their § petitions state that the woollen manufacture was *set up* in Ireland, as if it had been lately introduced there; and one of them goes so far as to represent the particular time and manner of introducing it. " Many of the poor of " that kingdom, says this extraordinary " petition, during the late rebellion there, " fled into the West of England, where " they were put to work in the woolen manu-

---

† Anderson on Com. 1 Vol. 131.

* The wish of traders for a monopoly is not confined to England; in the same kingdom some parts are restrained in favour of others, as in Sweden to this hour. Abbe Resnal. 2 Vol. 28.

§ Eng. Com. Journ. 12 Vol. 64, 68.

‡ Eng. Com. Jonrn. 12 Vol. 64.

"manufacture to learn that trade, and since the reduction of Ireland *endeavours were used* to *set up* those manufactures there."

Would any man suppose that this could relate to a manufacture, in which this kingdom excelled before the time of Edward the 3d, which had been the subject of so many laws in both kingdoms, and which was always cultivated here, and before this rebellion with more success than after it? the trading towns gave accounts totally inconsistent of the state of this manufacture at that time in England: from Exeter it is represented as greatly decayed and discouraged * in those parts, and diminished in England. But a petition from Leeds represents this manufacture as having very much increased† since the revolution in all its several branches, to the general interest of England; and yet, in two days after the clothiers from three towns in Gloucestershire assert, that the trade has decayed, and that the poor are almost starved ‡. The commissioners of trade differ in opinion from them, and by their

* English Com. Journ. vol. 12, p. 7.
† Ib. 527.   ‡ Ib. 530.

their report, it appears that the woollen manufacture was then very much increased and improved †. The traders have sometimes mistaken their own interests on those subjects; in 1698, a petition for prohibiting the importation from Ireland of all worsted and and woollen yarn, represents that the poor of England are ready to perish by this importation *; and in 1739, several petitions were preferred against taking off the duties § from worsted and bay yarn exported from Ireland to England. But this has been done in the manner before-mentioned, and is now acknowledged to be highly useful to England. Trading people have ever aimed at exclusive privileges; of this there are two extraordinary instances; in the year 1698, two petitions were preferred, from Folkstone and Aldborough, stating a singular grievance that they suffered from Ireland, " by the Irish catching herrings *at Waterford* " *and Wexford* ‡ and sending them to the " Streights, and thereby *forestalling* and ruin- " ing petitioners markets;" but these petitioners

† English Com. Jour. Vol. 12, p. 434.
*, Ib. 387.   § Ib. vol. 22.   ‡ Ib. 178.

oners had the *hard lot* of having motions in their favour rejected.

I wish that the fullest information may be had in this important investigation, but between the inconsistent accounts and opinions that will probably be given, experience only can decide; and experience will demonstrate that the removal of those restraints will promote the prosperity of both kingdoms.

I have the honour to be,

My lord, &c.

THE
COMMERCIAL RESTRAINTS
OF
IRELAND
CONSIDERED.

SIXTH LETTER.

THE COMMERCIAL RESTRAINTS OF IRELAND CONSIDERED.

SIXTH LETTER.

My Lord,

Dublin, 1st September, 1779.

By the proceedings in the English parliament in the year 1698, and the speech of the lords justices to the Irish parliament in that year it appears, that the linen was intended to be given to this country as an equivalent for the woollen manufacture. The opinion that this supposed equivalent was accepted of as such by Ireland is mistaken. The temperament, which the commons of Ireland in their address said they hoped to find, was no more than a partial and a temporary duty on the exportation,

exportation, as an experiment only, and not as an established system, reserving the exportation of frize, then much the most valuable part to Ireland §. The English intended the linen manufacture as a compensation, and declared they thought it would be much more advantageous to Ireland * than the woollen trade.

This idea of an equivalent has led several persons, and among the rest two very able writers †, into mistakes, from the want of information in some facts which are necessary to be known, that this transaction may be fully understood, and therefore ought to be particularly stated.

The

§ The lords commissioners of trade in England, by their report of the 31st August 1697, (Eng. Com. Jour. 12 vol. p. 428.) relating to the trade between England and Ireland, though they recommend the restraining of the exportation of all sorts of woollen manufactures out of Ireland, make the following exception, "except only, that of their "frize, as is wont, to England."
  * See before Speech of lords Justices.
  † Mr. Dobbs, and after him Dr. Smith.

The Irish had before this period applied themselves to the linen trade. This appears by two of their statutes, in the reign of Elizabeth, one laying a duty on the export of flax and linen yarn ‡, and the other, making it felony to ship them without paying such duty §. In the reign of Charles the 1st, great pains were taken by lord Strafford to encourage this manufacture; and in the succeeding reign †, the great and munificent efforts of the first duke of Ormond were crowned with merited success. The blasts of civil dissentions nipped those opening buds of industry, and when the season was more favourable, it is probable that, like England, they found the woollen manufacture a more useful object of national pursuit; which may be collected from the address of the English house of commons, " that they so unwillingly promote the linen " trade*;" and it was natural for a poor and exhausted

‡ 11 Elizabeth, session 3, ch. 10. § 13 Elizabeth, session 5, ch. 4. † 17 and 18 Ch. 2, ch. 9, for the advancement of the linen manufacture. Carte.

* See before.

exhausted country to work up the materials of which it was possessed.

In 1696 the English had given encouragement to the manufactures of hemp and flax in Ireland, but without stipulating any restraint of the export of woollen goods. The English act made in that year recites that great sums of money were yearly exported out of England, for the purchasing of hemp, flax and linen, and the productions thereof, which might be prevented by being supplied from Ireland, and allows natives of England and Ireland to import into England free of all duties §, hemp and flax, and all the productions thereof. In the same session ‡ a law passed in England for the more effectually preventing the exportation of wool, and for encouraging the importation thereof from Ireland. Both those manufactures were under the consideration of parliament this session, and it was thought, from enlarged views of the welfare of both kingdoms, that England should

§ 7 and 8 W. 3, ch. 39 from the 1st of August 1696.
‡ 7 and 8 W. ch. 28.

should encourage the linen, without discouraging the woollen manufacture of Ireland. There was no further encouragement given by England to our linen manufacture for some years after the year 1696*. *In 1699, there was no equivalent whatever given* for the prohibition of the export of our woollen manufactures.

It is true, the assurances given by both houses of parliament in England, for the encouragement of our linen trade, were as strong as words could express; but was this intended encouragement, if immediately carried into execution, an equivalent to Ireland for what she had lost? let it first be considered whether it was an equivalent at the time of the prohibition.

The woollen was then the principal manufacture and trade of Ireland. That it was then considered as her staple, appears from the several acts of parliament beforementioned

---

* Not till the year 1705.

mentioned, and from the attempt made in 1695, by the Irish house of commons, to lay a duty on all old and new drapery imported. The amount of the export proves § the value of the trade to so poor a country as Ireland, and makes it probable that she then clothed her own people. The address of the English house of lords shews that this manufacture was "growing" amongst us, and the goodness of our materials "for making *all manner* of cloth ‡." And the English act of 1698 is a voucher that this manufacture was then in so flourishing a state as to give apprehensions, however ill-founded, of its rivalling England in foreign markets. The immediate consequences to Ireland shewed the value of what she lost; many thousand manufacturers were obliged to leave this kingdom for want of employment; many parts of the southern and western counties were so far depopulated that they have not yet recovered a reasonable number of inhabitants; and the whole kingdom was reduced

§ Com. Jour. 2 Vol. 725, 733. 16. vol. 360.
‡ See before.

duced to the greatest poverty and distress*. The linen trade of Ireland was then of little consideration, compared with the woollen †. The whole exportation of linens in 1700 ‡ amounted only in value to 14,112l. It was an experiment substituted in the place of an established trade.

The English ports in Asia, Africa and America were then shut against our linens, and when they were opened § for our white and brown linens, the restraints of imports from thence to Ireland made that concession of less value, and she still found it her interest to send for the most part her linens to England. The linen could not have been a compensation for the woollen manufacture which employs by far a greater number of hands, and yields much greater profit to the public, as well as to the manufacturers ‖. Of this manufacture there are not many countries which have the primum in equal
perfection

* Dobbs 6, 7.   Com. Journ. 16 Vol. 362.
‡ Ib. 363.
§ By 3d and 4th Anne, ch. 9.
‖ And. on Comm. 2 Vol. 225.

perfection with England and Ireland, and no countries, taking in the various kinds of those extensive manufactures, so fit for carrying them on. There cannot be many rivals in this trade; in the linen they are most numerous. Other parts of the world are more fit for it than Ireland, and many equally so.

If this could be supposed to have been an equivalent at the time, or to have become so by its success, it can no longer be considered in that light. The commercial state of Europe is greatly altered. Ireland can no longer enjoy the benefit intended for her. It was intended that the great sums of money remitted out of England to foreign countries in this branch of commerce should all center in Ireland, and that England should be supplied with linen from thence*; but foreigners now draw great sums from England in this trade, and rival the

---

* This appears by the preamble to the English act of the 7th and 8th W. III. c. 39.

the Irish in the English markets. The Russians are become powerful rivals to the Irish and underfel them in the coarfe kinds of linen. This is now the ftaple manufacture of Scotland. England that had formerly cultivated this manufacture without fuccefs, and had taken linens * from France to the amount of 700,000l. yearly, has now made great progrefs in it. The encouragement of this trade in England and Scotland has been long a principal object to the British legiflature, and the nation that encouraged us to the undertaking is now become our rival in it †; that this is not too ftrong an expreffion will appear by confidering two British ftatutes, one of which ‡ has laid a duty on the importation of Irish fail-cloth into Great-Britain, as long as the bounties fhould be paid on the exportation from § Ireland, which obliged us to
discontinue

---

* Anderfon on Commerce, 2 Vol. 177.
† Com. Journ. 16 Vol. 365.
‡ In 1750.
§ By the law of 1750, and the bounties given on the
exportation

discontinue them; and the other* has given a bounty on the exportation of *British* chequered and striped linens exported out of *Great-Britain* to Africa, America, Spain, Portugal, Gibraltar, the island of Minorca, or the East-Indies. This is now become a very valuable part of the manufacture, which Great-Britain by the operation of this bounty keeps to herself. The bounties on the exportation of all other linen, which she has generously given to ours as well as to her own † operate much more strongly in favour of the latter‡; the expence of freight, insurance, commission, &c. in sending

exportation of sail-cloth from Great-Britain to foreign countries, Ireland has almost lost this trade; she cannot now supply herself. Great-Britain has not been the gainer; the quantities of sail-cloth imported there in 1774, exceeding, according to the return from the custom-house in London, the quantities imported in the year 1750, when the restrictive law was made. It has been taken from Ireland, and given to the Russians, Germans, and Dutch. Ir. Com. Journ 16 Vol. 363.

* 10 G. III. ch.   continued by act of last session to the year 1786.

† In the year 1743.

‡ Com. Journ. 16 Vol. 369, 389.

sending the linens from Ireland to England has been computed at four per cent. and, if this computation is right, when the British linens obtain 12l. per cent. the full amount of the premium, the Irish do not receive above eight. Those bounties, though acknowledged to be a favour to Ireland, give Great-Britain a further, and a very important advantage in this trade, by inducing us to send all our linens to England, from whence other countries are supplied.

The great hinge upon which the stipulation on the part of England in the year 1698 turned, was that England should give every possible encouragement to the linen and hempen manufactures in Ireland. Encouraging these manufactures in another country was not compatible with this intention. The course of events made it necessary to do this in Scotland*; the course of trade

---

* *To please the English* Scotland has for half a century past exerted herself, as much as possible, to improve the linen manufacture. Anderson on Industry, 2 Vol. 233.

trade made it neceffary for England to do the fame; a commercial country muft cultivate every confiderable manufacture of which fhe has or can get the primum. Thefe circumftances have totally changed the ftate of the queftion; and if it was reafonable and juft that Ireland in 1698 fhould have accepted of the linen in the place of the woollen manufactures, it deferves to be confidered, whether by the almoft total change of the circumftances it is not now unreafonable and unjuft.

America itfelf, the opening of whofe markets‡ to Irifh linens was thought to have been one of the principal encouragements to that trade, is now become a rival and an enemy, and when fhe puts off the latter character will appear in the former with new force and infinite advantages.

The emigrations for many years of fuch great multitudes of our linen manufacturers
to

‡ Com. Journ. 16 vol. p. 370.

LET. 6.   OF IRELAND CONSIDERED.   141

to America * proves incontrovertibly that they can carry on their trade with more fuccefs in America than in Ireland. But let us examine the facts to determine whether the propofed encouragements have taken place. The declaration of the lords of England for the encouragement of the linen manufacture of Ireland was, " to all the " advantage and profit that kingdom can be " capable of," and of the commons, " that " they fhall be *always* ready to give it their " *utmoft* affiftance." The fpeech of the lords juftices fhews the extent of this engagement, and promifes the encouragement of England, " to the linen and hempen " manufactures of Ireland."

In the year 1705† liberty was given to the natives of England or Ireland, to export from Ireland to the Englifh plantations white and brown linens only, but no liberty given

* The province of Ulfter in two years is faid to have loft 30.000 of its inhabitants. Com. Journ. 16 v. 381.

† From 24th June 1705. 3 and 4 Ann ch. 8. for 11 years; but afterwards continued.

given to bring in return any goods from thence to Ireland, which will appear, from the account in the appendix, to have made this law of inconfiderable effect. In 1743 premiums were given on the exportation of Englifh and Irifh linens from Great Britain, and the bounty granted by Great Britain in 1774, on flax-feed imported into Ireland, is a further proof of the munificent attention of Great Britain to our linen trade. But checquered, ftriped, printed, painted, ftained or dyed linens were not until lately admitted into the plantations from Ireland; and the ftatutes of queen Anne*, laying duties at the rate of 30 per cent on fuch linens made in *foreign* parts and imported into Great Britain, have been, rather by a forced conftruction, extended to Ireland, which is deprived of the Britifh markets † for thofe goods, and, until the year 1777 ‡, was excluded from the American markets alfo.

* Brit. acts, 10 Anne, ch. 19. 11 and 12 Anne, ch. 9. 6 G. 1, ch. 4.
† Brit. act, 18 G. 3, ch. 53.
‡ Ir. Com. Journ. 16 vol. 363, 364.

also. But it is thought as to checquered and striped linens, which are a valuable branch of the linen trade, that this act will have little effect in favour of this country, from the operation of the before-mentioned British act of the 10th G. 3, which, by granting a bounty on the exportation of those goods of the manufacture of Great Britain only, gives a direct preference to the British linen manufacture before the Irish.

The hempen manufacture of Ireland has been so far *discouraged* by Great Britain, that the Irish have totally abandoned the culture of hemp*.

I hope to be excused for weighing scrupulously a proposed equivalent, for which the receiver was obliged to part with the advantages of which he was possessed. The equivalent, given in 1667 for the almost entire exclusion of Ireland from the ports of England and America, was the exportation of

* Ir. Com. Journ. 16 vol. 365.

of our manufactures to foreign nations. The prohibition of 1699 was not altogether consistent with the equivalent of 1667; and from the equivalent of 1698 the superior encouragement since given to English and Scotch linen, and the discouragement to the checquer and stamped linen and sail cloth of Ireland must make a large deduction. But why must one manufacture only be encouraged? the linen and the woollen trades of Ireland were formerly both encouraged by the legiflatures of both kingdoms; they are now both equally encouraged in England.

If this single trade was found sufficient employment for 1,000,000 men who remained in this country at the time of this restraint (the contrary of which has been shewn), it would require the interposition of more than human wisdom to divide it among 2,500,000 men at this day, and to send the multitude away satisfied.

No populous commercial country can subsist on one manufacture; if the world has

has ever produced such an instance, I have not been able to find it. Reason and experience demonstrate that, to make a society happy, the members of it must be able to supply the wants of each other, as far as their country affords the means, and where it does not, by exchanging the produce of their industry for that of their neighbours. Where the former is discouraged or the latter prevented, that community cannot be happy. If they are not allowed to send to other countries the manufactured produce of their own, the people who enjoy that liberty will undersell them in their own markets; the restrained manufacturers will be reduced to poverty, and will hang like paralytic limbs on the rest of the body.

If England's commercial system would have been incomplete, had she failed to cultivate any one principal manufacture of which she had or could obtain the material, what shall we say to the commercial state of that country, restrained in a manufacture of which she has the materials in abundance,

bundance, and in which she had made great progress, and almost confined to one manufacture of which she has not the primum.

Manufactures, though they may flourish for a time, generally fail in countries that do not produce the principal materials of them. Of this there are many instances. Venice and the other Italian states carried on the woollen manufacture, until the countries which produced the materials manufactured them, when the Italian manufactures declined, and dwindled into little consideration in comparison of their former splendor. The Flemings, from their vicinity to those countries that produced the materials, beat the Italians out of their markets. But when England cultivated that manufacture, the Flemings lost it. That this and not oppression was the cause appears from the flourishing state of the linen manufacture* there, because it consumes flax the native

---

* Anderson on Industry, 1 vol. 34 to 40.

native produce of the foil; and it is much to be feared that thofe iflands will be obliged to yield the fuperiority in this trade to other nations that have great extent of country, and fufficient land to fpare for this impoverifhing production.

That fome parts of Ireland may produce good flax muft be allowed, and alfo that parts of Flanders would produce fine wool. But though the legiflature has for many years made it a capital object to encourage the growth of flax and the raifing of flax-feed in this kingdom, yet it is obliged to pay above 9000l. yearly in premiums on the importation of flax-feed, which is now almoft all imported, and cofts us between 70 and 80,000l. yearly. Flax-farming, in any large quantity, is become a precarious and lofing trade†, and thofe who have been induced to attempt it by premiums from the linen-board have, after receiving thofe premiums,

† Com. Journ. 16 vol. 370.

miums, generally found themselves losers, and have declined that branch of tillage.

When the imported flax-seed is unsound and fails in particular districts, which very frequently happens, the distress, confusion and litigation that arise among manufacturers, farmers, retailers and merchants, affords a melancholy proof of the dangerous consequences to a populous nation, when the industry of the people, and the hope of the rising year rest on a single manufacture, for the materials of which we must depend upon the courtesy and good faith of other nations.

Let me appeal to the experience of very near a century, in the very instance now before you. A single manufacture is highly encouraged; it obtains large premiums not only from the legislature of its own country, but from that of a great neighbouring kingdom; it becomes not only the first, but almost the sole national object; immense sums of money are expended in the cultivation

tion of it §, and the fuccefs exceeds our moſt ſanguine expectations. But look into the ſtate of this country; you will find property circulating flowly and languidly, and in the moſt numerous claſſes of your people, no circulation or property at all. You will frequently find them in want of employment and of food, and reduced in a vaſt number of inſtances from the flighteſt cauſes to diſtreſs and beggary. All other manufacturers will continue ſpiritleſs, poor and diſtreſſed, and derive from uncertain employment a precarious and miſerable ſubſiſtence; they gain little by the fuccefs of the proſperous trade, the dealers in which are tempted to buy from that country to which they principally fell; the diſeaſe of thoſe morbid parts muſt ſpread through the whole body, and will at length reach the perſons employed in the favoured manufacture. Theſe will become poor and wretched and diſcontented; they emigrate by thouſands; in vain you repreſent the crime of

deſerting

§ See Com. Jour. 17 vol. 263 to 267 for the ſums paid from 1700 to 1775. They amount to 803,4861 0s 2¾ d

deserting their country, the folly of forsaking their friends, the temerity of wandering to distant and perhaps inhospitable climates; their despondency is deaf to the suggestions of prudence, and will answer, that they can no longer stay " where hope never comes," but will fly from these " regions of sorrow*."

Let me not be thought to undervalue the bounties and generosity of that great nation which has taken our linen trade under its protection. There is much ill-breeding, though perhaps some good sense, in the churlish reply of the philosopher to the request of the prince who visited his humble dwelling, and desired to know, and to gratify his wishes; they were no more than this, that the prince should not stand between the philosopher and the sun. Had he been a man of the world he might have expressed the same idea with more address, though with less force and significance; he

---

* This malady of emigration among our linen manufacturers has appeared at many different periods during this century.

he might have said, "I am sensible of your greatness and of your power; I have no doubts of your liberality; but Nature has abundantly given me all that I wish; intercept not one of her greatest gifts; allow me to enjoy the bounties of her hand, and the contentment of my own mind will furnish the rest."

I have the honour to be,

My lord, &c.

THE
COMMERCIAL RESTRAINTS
OF
IRELAND
CONSIDERED.

SEVENTH LETTER.

THE
COMMERCIAL RESTRAINTS
OF
IRELAND
CONSIDERED.

SEVENTH LETTER.

My Lord,

Dublin, 3d Sept. 1779.

BY comparing the reftrictive law of 1699, with the ftatutes which had been previoufly enacted in England from the 15th year of the reign of Charles the fecond, relative to the Colonies, it appears that this reftrictive law originated in a fyftem of colonization. The principle of that fyftem was that the Colonies fhould fend their materials to England and take from thence her manufactures, and that the making thofe manufactures in the Colonies fhould be prohibited

hibited or discouraged. But was it reasonable to extend this principle to Ireland? the climate, growth and productions of the Colonies were different from those of their parent country. England had no sugar canes, coffee, dying stuff, and little tobacco. She took all those from her Colonies only, and it was thought reasonable that they should take from her only the manufactures which she made. But in Ireland, the climate, soil, growth and productions are the same as in England, who could give no such equivalent to Ireland as she gave to America, and was so far from considering her, when this system first prevailed, as a proper subject for such regulations, that she was allowed the benefits arising from those Colonies equally with England, until the 15th year of the reign of king Charles * the second. By an act passed in that year Ireland had no longer the privilege of sending any of her exports, except servants, horses, victuals and salt, to any of the Colonies;

* 15 Ch. II. ch. 7.

nies; the reasons are assigned in the preamble, " to make this kingdom a staple, not
" only of the commodities of those planta-
" tions, but also of the commodities of other
" countries and places for the supplying of
" them, and it being the usage of other na-
" tions to keep their plantation trade to
" themselves *." At the time of passing this
law, though less liberal ideas in respect of Ireland were then entertained, it went no further than not to extend to her the benefit of those Colony regulations; but it was not then thought that this kingdom was a proper subject for any such regulations. The scheme of substituting there, instead of the woollen, the linen trade, was not at that time thought of. The English were desirous to establish it among themselves, and by an act of parliament † made in that year for encouraging the manufacture of linen, granted to all foreigners who shall set it up
in

---

* As other nations did the same, Ireland was shut out from the new world, and a considerable part of the old in Asia and Africa.

† 15 Ch. II. ch. 15.

in England, the privileges of natural born subjects.

But it appears by the English statute of the 7th and 8th Will. III*. which has been before stated, that this scheme had not succeeded in England, and from this act it is manifest that England considered itself as well as Ireland interested to encourage the linen-manufacture there; and it does not then appear to have been thought just, that Ireland should purchase this benefit for both, by giving up the exportation of any other manufacture. But in 1698 a different principle prevailed; in effect the same, so far as relates to the woollen manufacture, with that which had prevailed as to the commerce of the Colonies. This is evident from the preamble of the English law † made in 1699, " for as much as wool and woollen manu- " factures of cloth, serge, bays, kerfies and " other stuffs, made or mixed with wool,
" are

* Ch. 39.
† 10th and 11th W. III. ch. 10.

" are the greatest, and most profitable com-
" modities of this kingdom, on which the
" value of lands and the trade of the nation
" do chiefly depend, and whereas great quan-
" tities of like manufactures have of late
" been made and are daily encreasing in the
" kingdom of Ireland, and *in the English*
" *plantations* in America, and are exported
" from thence to foreign markets, hereto-
" fore supplied from England, which will
" inevitably sink the value of lands, and
" tend to the ruin of the trade and woollen
" manufactures of this realm; for the pre-
" vention whereof and for the encourage-
" ment of the woollen manufactures in this
" kingdom, &c."

The ruinous consequences of the woollen manufactures of Ireland to the value of lands, trade and manufactures of England, stated in this act, are apprehensions that were entertained, and not events that had happened; and before those facts are taken for granted, I request the mischiefs recited in the acts* made in England to prevent the importation of cattle dead or alive from Ireland, may be confidered. The mifchiefs ftated in thofe feveral laws are fuppofed to be as ruinous to England as thofe recited in the act of 1699, and yet are now allowed to be groundlefs apprehenfions, occafioned by fhort and miftaken views of the real intereft of England. Sir W. Petty † demonftrates that the opinion entertained in England at the time of his prohibition of the import of cattle from Ireland was ill-founded; he calls it a ftrange conceit. If he was now living, he would probably confider the prohibition of our woollen exports as not having a much better foundation.

Connecting

* 15 Ch. II. ch. 7. 18 Ch. II. ch. 2. 20 Ch. II. ch. 7. 22d and 23d Ch. II. ch. 2. 32 Ch. II. ch. 2.

† Petty's Political Survey of Ireland, 70 ; and ib. Report from the Council of Trade, 117, 118.

Sir W. Temple, 3 Vol. p. 22, 23, that England was evidently a lofer by the prohibition of Cattle.

Dr. Smith's Memoirs of Wool, 2 Vol. 337, that the Englifh had fince fufficiently felt the mifchiefs of this proceeding.

Connecting this preamble of the act of 1699, with the speech made from the throne to the parliament of Ireland in the year 1698, with the addresses of both houses in England, and with the prohibition, by this and by other acts formerly made in England, of exporting wool from Ireland except to that kingdom, the object of this new commercial regulation is obvious. It was to discourage the woollen manufacture in Ireland, and in effect, to prohibit the exportation from thence, because it was the principal branch of manufacture and trade in England, to induce us to send to them our materials for that manufacture, and that we should be supplied with it by them, and to encourage, as a compensation to Ireland, the linen manufacture, which was not at that time a commercial object of any importance to England. This I take to be a part of the system of colony regulations. Whether it was reasonable or just to bring this kingdom into that system, has been already submitted from arguments drawn from the climates and productions of the different countries.

M

countries. The supposed compensation was no more than what Ireland had before; no further encouragement was given by England to our linen manufacture until six years after this prohibition, when at the request of the Irish house of commons, and after a representation of the ruinous state of this country, liberty was given by an English act of parliament * to export our white and brown linens into the colonies, which was allowing us to do as to one manufacture what, before the 15th of king Charles the second, was permitted in every instance.

It would be presumption in a private man to decide on the weight of those arguments; but to select and arrange facts that lie dispersed in journals and books of statutes in both kingdoms, and to make observations on those facts with caution and respect, can never give offence to those who inquire for the purpose of relieving a distressed

---

* 3 and 4 Ann. ch. 8.

tressed nation, and of promoting the general welfare.

In that confidence I beg leave to place this subject in a different view, and to request that it may be considered what the commercial system of this kingdom was at the time of passing this law of 1699? and whether it was, in this respect, reasonable or just that such a regulation should have been then made? The great object which the lords and commons of Great Britain have determined to investigate lead to such a discussion; determined as they are to pursue effectual methods " for promoting " the common strength, wealth and com- " merce of both kingdoms," what better guides can they follow than the examples of their ancestors, and the means used by them for many centuries, and in the happiest times, for attaining the same great purposes.

In my opinion it would be improper, in the present state of the British empire, to

agitate

agitate disputed questions that may enflame the passions of men. May no such questions ever arise between two affectionate sister kingdoms! It is my purpose only to state acknowledged facts, which never have been contested, and from those facts to lay before you the commercial system of Ireland before the year 1699.

For several centuries before this period Ireland was in possession of the English common law *, and of magna charta. The former secures the subject in the enjoyment of property of every kind; and by the latter *the liberties of all the ports of the kingdom are established.*

The statutes made in England for the common and public weal, are † by an Irish act of the 10th of Henry the 7th, made laws

---

* 4 Inst. 349. Matth. Paris, anno 1172. p. 121, 220. Vit. H. 2. Pryn. against the 4th Inst. c. 76, p. 250, 252. Sir John Davis's Hist. 71. Lord Lyttleton's Hist. of H. 2. 3 Vol. 89, 90. 7 Co. 22. 23. 4th Black. 429.
Cooke's 4th Inst. 351.

laws in Ireland; and the English commercial statutes, in which Ireland is expresly mentioned, will place the former state of commerce in this country in a light very different from that in which it has been generally considered in Great-Britain.

By the 17th of Edward the 3d, ch. 1. all sorts of merchandizes may be exported from Ireland, except to the king's enemies.

By the 27th of Edward the 3d, ch. 18. merchants of Ireland and Wales may bring their merchandize to the staple of England; and by the 34th of the same king, ch. 17. all kinds of merchandizes may be exported from and imported into Ireland, as well by aliens as denizens. In the same year there is another statute, ch. 18. that all persons who have lands or possessions in Ireland, might freely import thither, and export from that kingdom *their own commodities*; and by the 50th of Edward the 3d, ch. 8. no alnage is to be paid, if frize ware, which are made in Ireland.

This

This freedom of commerce was beneficial to both countries. It enabled Ireland to be very serviceable to Edward the 3d, as it had been to his father and grandfather, in supplying numbers of armed vessels for transporting their great lords and their attendants and troops * to Scotland, and also to Portsmouth for his French wars.

But the reign of Edward the 4th furnishes still stronger instances of the regard shewn by England to the trade and manufactures of this country.

In the third year of that monarch's reign the artificers of England complained to parliament that they were greatly impoverished and *could not live* by bringing in divers commodities and wares ready wrought †. An act passed reciting those complaints and ordaining that no merchant born a subject of the king, denizen or stranger, or other person should bring into England or Wales any

---

* Anderson on Commerce, 1 Vol. 174.
† 3d Edw. 4. ch. 4.

any woollen cloths, &c. and enumerates many other manufactures, on pain of forfeiture; provided that all wares and "chaffers" made and wrought in Ireland or Wales, may be brought in and fold in t e realm of England, as they were wont before the making of that act *.

In the next year another act † paffed in that kingdom, that all woollen cloth brought into England and fet to fale, fhould be forfeited, except cloths made in Wales or Ireland.

In thofe reigns England was as careful of the commerce and manufactures of her ancient fifter kingdom, particularly in her great ftaple trade, as fhe was of her own.

Of this attention there were further inftances in the years 1468 and 1478. In two treaties

---

* The part of this law which mentions that it fhall be determinable at the king's pleafure, has the prohibition for its object, and does not leffen the force of the argument in favour of Ireland.

† 4th Edw. IV. ch. 1.

treaties concluded in those years between England and the duke of Bretagne, the merchandize to be traded in between England, Ireland and Calais on the one part, and Bretagne on the other, is specified, and woollen cloths are particularly mentioned*.

And in a treaty between Henry the 7th and the Netherlands, Ireland is included, both as to exports and imports †.

The commercial acts of parliament in which Ireland is mentioned have only been stated, because they are not generally known. But the laws made in England before the 10th of Henry the 7th, for the protection of merchants and the security of trade, being laws for the common and public weal, are also made laws here by the Irish statute of that year, which was returned under the great seal of England, and must have been previously considered in the privy council of that kingdom. At this period then the

English

---

* Anderson on Commerce, 1 Vol. 285.
† Ib. 319.

English commercial system and the Irish, so far as it depended upon the English statute law, was the same; and before this period, so far as it depended upon the common law and Magna Charta, was also the same.

From that time until the 15th of king Charles the 2d, which takes in a period of 167 years, the commercial constitution of Ireland was as much favoured and protected as that of England; " the free enlargement " of common traffick which his majesty's " subjects of Ireland enjoyed," is taken notice of, incidentally, in an English statute, in the reign of king James the 1st*; and in 1627 king Charles the 1st made a strong declaration in favour of the trade and manufactures of this country. By several English statutes in the reign of king Charles the 2d, an equal attention was shewn to the woollen manufactures in both kingdoms; in the 12th year of his reign† the exportation of wool, wool-felts, fuller's earth, or any kind of

---

* 3d James, ch. 6.
† 12th Ch. 2, ch. 32.

of scowering-earth, was prohibited from both. But let the reasons, mentioned in the preamble, for passing this law be adverted to, —" for preventing inconveniencies "and losses that happened, and that daily "do and may happen to the kingdom of "England, dominion of Wales, and king- "dom of Ireland, through the secret expor- "tation of wool out of and from the said "kingdoms and dominions; and for the *better* "*setting on work the poor people* and inhabi- "tants of the kingdoms and dominions "aforesaid, and to the intent that the full "use and benefit of *the principal native com-* "*modities* of the same kingdom and domini- "on may come, redound and be unto the "subjects and inhabitants of the same:"

This was the voice of nature, and the dictate of sound and general policy; it proclaimed to the nations that they should not give to strangers the bread of their own children, that the produce of the soil should support the inhabitants of the country, that their industry should be exercised on their own

own materials, and that the poor should be employed, clothed and fed.

The shipping and navigation of England and Ireland were at this time equally favoured and protected. By another act of the same year no goods or commodities † of the growth, production or manufacture of Asia, Africa or America, shall be imported into England, *Ireland* or Wales, but in ships which belong to the people of England or *Ireland*, the dominion of Wales, or the town of Berwick upon Tweed, or which are of the built of the said lands, and of which the master and three-fourths of the mariners are English; and a subsequent statute * makes the encouragement to navigation in both countries equal, by ordaining that the subjects of Ireland and of the Plantations shall be accounted English within the meaning of that clause. Another law ‡ of the same reign shews that the navigation

† 12 Ch. 2, ch. 18.
* 13th and 14th Ch. 2, ch. 11.
‡ 13th and 14th Ch. 2, ch. 18.

vigation, commerce and woollen manufactures of both kingdoms were equally protected by the English legislature. This act lays on the same restraint as the abovementioned act of the 12th of Charles 2d. and makes the transgression still more penal. It recites that wool, wool-felts, &c. are secretly exported from England and Ireland to foreign parts to the great decay of the woollen manufactures and the destruction of the navigation and commerce of *these kingdoms*.

From those laws it appears that the commerce, navigation and manufactures of this country were not only favoured and protected by the English legislature, but that we had in those times the full benefit of their Plantation trade; whilst the woollen manufactures were protected and encouraged in England and Ireland, the planting of tobacco in both was prohibited, because " it " was one of the main products of several " of the plantations, and upon which their
welfare

" welfare and subsistence do depend †. This policy was liberal, just and equal, it opened the resources and cultivated the strength of every part of the empire.

This commercial system of Ireland was enforced by several acts of her own legislature; two statutes passed in the reign of Henry the 8th to prevent the exportation of wool, because, says the first of those laws, " it hath been the cause of dearth of " cloth and idleness of many folks*," and " tends to the desolation and ruin of this " poor land." The second of those laws inforces the prohibition § by additional penalties; it recites, " that the said beneficial " law had taken little effect, but that since " the making thereof great plenty of wool " had been conveyed out of this land to the " great and inestimable hurt, decay and im- " poverishment of the king's poor subjects " within the said land, for redress whereof " and in consideration that conveying of the
" wool

† 12 Ch. 2, ch. 27.
* Ir. act, 13 H. 8, ch. 2.   § 28 H. 8, ch. 17.

" wool of the growth of this land out of
" the fame is one of the greateſt occaſions
" of the idleneſs of the people, waſte, ruin
" and defolation of the king's cities and bo-
" rough towns, and other places of his do-
" minion within this land." The 11th of
Elizabeth* lays duties on the exportation
equal to a prohibition; and the reaſon given
in the preamble ought to be mentioned;
" that the ſaid commodities may be more
" abundantly wrought in this realm ere they
" ſhall be ſo tranſported, than preſently they
" are, which ſhall ſet many now living idle
" on work, to the great relief and commodity
" of this realm†.

By the preamble of one of thoſe acts §, made in the reign of Charles the Second, it appears that the ſale of Iriſh woollen goods
in

* Ch. 10.
† The neceſſity of encouraging the people of Ireland to manufacture their own wool, appears by divers ſtatutes to have been the ſenſe of the legiſlature of both kingdoms for ſome centuries.
§ Ir. Act of 17 and 18 Ch. 2, ch. 15.

in foreign markets was encouraged by England; " whereas there is a general complaint
" in *England,* France, and other parts be-
" yond the seas, (whither the woollen cloths
" and other commodities made of wool in
" this his majesty's kingdom of Ireland are
" transported) of the false, deceitful, uneven,
" and uncertain making thereof, which com-
" eth to pass by reason that the clothiers
" and makers thereof do not observe any
" certain assize for length, breath and
" weight for making their clothes and other
" commodities aforesaid in this kingdom, as
" they do in the realm of England, and as
" they ought also to do here; by which
" means the merchants, buyers and users of
" the said cloth and other commodities are
" much abused and deceived, and the credit,
" esteem and sale of the said cloth and com-
" modities is thereby much impaired and un-
" dervalued, to the great and general hurt
" and hindrance of the trade of clothing in
" this whole realm."

After

After the ports of England were shut against our cattle, and our trade to the English colonies was restrained, still this commercial system was adhered to by encouraging the manufactures of this country, and the exportation of them to foreign countries. In 1667, when the power of the crown was not so well understood as at present, the proclamation before mentioned was published by the lord lieutenant and privy council of Ireland*, in pursuance of a letter from Charles the Second, by the advice of his council in England, notifying to all his subjects of this kingdom, the allowance of a free trade to all foreign countries, either at war or peace with his majesty.

In the year 1663 the distinctions between the trade of England and Ireland †, and the restraints on that of the latter commenced. By an English act passed in that year, intitled an act " for the encouragement of
" trade,"

* Carte, 2 Vol. p. 344.
† 15 Ch. 2, ch. 7.

"trade," a title not very applicable to the parts of it that related to Ireland, besides laying a duty nearly equal to a prohibition on cattle imported into England from that kingdom, the exportation of all commodities, except victuals, servants, horses, and salt for the fisheries of New England and Newfoundland, from thence to the English plantations, was prohibited from the 25th of March, 1764. The exports allowed were useful to them, but prejudicial to Ireland, as they consisted of our people, our provisions, and a material for manufacture which we might have used more profitably on our own coasts.

In 1670 another act * passed in England, to prohibit from the 24th of March 1671 the exportation from the English plantations to Ireland of several materials for manufactures †, without first unloading in England or

---

* 22d and 23d Ch. 2d, ch. 26.

† Sugar, tobacco, cotton, wool, indigo, steel or Jamaica wood, fustick, or other dying wood, the growth of the said plantations.

or Wales. We are informed by this act that the restraint of the exportation from the English plantations to Ireland was intended by the act of 1663; but the intention is not effectuated, though the importation of those commodities into Ireland *from England*, without first unloading there, is, in effect, prohibited by that act.

The prohibition of importing into Ireland any plantation goods, unless the same had been first landed in England, and had paid the duties, is made general, without any exception, by the English act of the 7th and 8th W. 3d, ch. 22.

But by subsequent British acts*, it is made lawful to import from his majesty's plantations, all goods of their growth or manufactures, the articles enumerated in those several acts excepted†.

By

---

* 4 Geo. 2, ch. 15.   6 G. 2, ch. 15.   4 G. 2, ch. 15.
† The articles in the last note, and also rice, molasses, beaver skins and other furs, copper ore, pitch, tar, turpentine,

By a late British act[‡] there is a considerable extension of the exports from Ireland to the British plantations. But it is apprehended that this law will not answer the kind intentions of the British legislature. Denying the import from those countries to Ireland, is, in effect, preventing the export from

tine, masts, yards and bowsprits, pimento, cocoa nuts, whale fins, raw silk, hides and skins, pot and pearl ashes, iron and lumber.

[‡] From the 24th of June 1778, it shall be lawful to export from Ireland directly into any of the British plantations in America, or the West Indies, or into any of the settlements belonging to Great Britain on the coast of Africa, any goods being the produce or manufacture of Ireland (wool and woollen manufactures in all its branches, mixed or unmixed, cotton manufactures of all sorts mixed or unmixed, hats, glass, hops, gun-powder and coals, only excepted) and all goods, &c. of the growth, produce or manufacture of Great Britain, which may be legally imported from thence into Ireland (woollen manufactures in all its branches, and glass, excepted) and all foreign certificate goods that may be legally imported from Great Britain into Ireland. Two of the principal manufactures are excepted, and one of them closely connected with, if not a part of the linen manufacture.—18 Geo. 3, ch. 55.

from Ireland to those countries. Money cannot be expected for our goods there; we must take theirs in exchange, and this can never anſwer on the terms of our being obliged, in our return, to paſs by Ireland, to land thoſe goods in England, to ſhip them a ſecond time, and then to ſail back again to Ireland. No trade will bear ſuch an unneceſſary delay and expence. The quickneſs and the ſecurity of the return are the great inducements to every trade. One is loſt and the other hazarded by ſuch embarraſſments; thoſe who are not ſubject to them carry on the trade with ſuch advantages over thoſe who are ſo entangled, as totally to exclude them from it. This is no longer the ſubject of ſpeculation, it has been proved by the experience of above ſeventy years. Since the year 1705, when liberty was given to import white and brown linens from Ireland into the Engliſh plantations, the quantities ſent there directly from Ireland were at all times very inconſiderable; notwithſtanding this liberty they were ſent for the moſt part from Ireland to England,

England, before any bounty was given on the exportation from thence, which did not take place until the year 1743, and from England the Englifh plantations were fupplied. There cannot be a more decifive proof that the liberty of exporting without a direct import in return, will not be beneficial to Ireland.

This country is the part of the Britifh empire moft conveniently fituated for trade with the colonies; if not fuffered to have any beneficial intercourfe with them, fhe will be deprived of one of the great advantages of her fituation; and fuch an obftruction to the profperity of fo confiderable a part, muft neceffarily diminifh the ftrength of the whole Britifh empire.

Thofe laws laid Ireland under reftraints highly prejudicial to her commerce and navigation. From thofe countries the materials for fhip-building *, and fome of thofe
 ufed

* This appears by the Englifh acts (3 and 4 Ann. ch. 10. 8 Ann. ch. 13. 2 Geo 2d, ch. 35.) giving bounties on the importation of thofe articles into Great Britain.

used in perfecting their staple manufactures were had; Ireland was by those laws excluded from almost all the trade of three quarters of the globe, and from all direct beneficial intercourse with her fellow-subjects in those countries, which were partly stocked from her own loins. But still, though deprived at that time of the benefit of those colonies, she was not then considered as a colony herself; her manufacturers were not in any other manner discouraged, her ports were left open, and she was at liberty to look for a market among strangers, though not among her fellow-subjects in Asia, Africa or America *. By the law of 1699 she

---

* Sir William Petty mentions that " the English who have " lands in Ireland were forced to trade only with strangers, " and became unacquainted with their own country, and " that England gained more than it lost by a free com- " merce (with Ireland), as exporting hither three times " as much as it received from hence;" and mentions his surprize at their being debarred from bringing commodities from America directly home, and being obliged to bring them round from England with extreme hazard and loss.—Political Survey of Ireland, p. 123.

LET. 7.   OF IRELAND CONSIDERED.   183

she was, as to her staple manufacture, deprived of those resources; she was brought within a system of colonization, but on worse terms than any of the plantations who were allowed to trade with each other †.

She could send her principal materials for manufacture to England only; but those manufactures were encouraged in England and discouraged in Ireland. The probable consequence of which was, and the event has answered the expectation, that we should take those manufactures from that country, and that therefore in those various trades which employ the greatest numbers of men, the English should work for our people. The rich should work for the poor!

Let the histories of both kingdoms, and the statute books of both parliaments be examined, and no precedent will be found

for

† 22d and 23d Ch. 2d, ch. 26. Sec. 11.

for the act of 1699, or for the fyftem which it introduced.

The whole tenor of the Englifh ftatutes relative to the trade of this country, and which by our act of the 10th of Hen. VII. became a part of our commercial conftitution, breath a fpirit totally repugnant to the principle of that law, and it is therefore with the utmoft deference fubmitted to thofe who have the power to decide, whether this law was agreeable to the commercial conftitution of Ireland, which for 500 years has never produced a fimilar inftance.

It might be naturally fuppofed, by a perfon not verfed in our ftory, that in the feventeenth century there had been fome offence given, or fome demerit on our part. He would be furprized to hear that during this period our loyalty had been exemplary, and our fufferings on that account great. In 1641, great numbers of the proteftants of Ireland were deftroyed, and many of them were

were deprived of their property, and driven out of their country from their attachment to the English government in this kingdom, and to that religion and conftitution which they happily enjoyed under it. At the revolution they were conftant in the fame principles, and fuccefsfully ftaked their lives and properties againft domeftick and foreign enemies, in fupport of the rights of the English crown, and of the religious and civil liberties of Britain and of Ireland. They bravely fhared with her in all her dangers, and liberally partook of all her adverfities. Whatever were their rights they had forfeited none of them. Whatever favours they enjoyed, they had new claims, from their merit and their fufferings, to a continuance of them. They now wanted more than ever the care of that foftering hand, which by refcuing them twice from oppreffion (obligations never to be forgotten by the proteftants of Ireland) eftablifhed the liberties, confirmed the ftrength, and raifed the glory of the Britifh empire.

In speaking of a commercial system it is not intended to touch upon the power of making or altering laws; the present subject leads us only to consider whether that power has been exercised, in any instances, contrary to reason, justice, and public utility,

When we consider, with the utmost deference to established authority, what is *reasonable, useful and just*, principles equally applicable to an independent or a subordinate, to a rich or a poor country—

Quod æque pauperibus prodest, locupletibus æque.—

Should any man talk of a conquest above 500 years since, between kingdoms long united, like those, in blood, interest and constitution, he does not speak to the purpose; he may as well talk of the conquest of the Norman, and use the antiquated language of obsolete despotism. I revere that conquest which has given to Ireland the common law and the Magna Charta of England.

When we confider what is *reafonable, ufeful and juft*, and addrefs our fentiments to a nation renowned for wifdom a: d juftice, fhould pride pervert the queftion, talk of the power of Britain, and in the character of that great country, afk, like Tancred, who fhall controul me? I anfwer, like the fober Siffredi——*thyfelf.*

The power of regulating trade in a great empire is perverted, when exercifed for the deftruction of trade in any part of it; but whatever or wherever that power is, if it fays to the fubject on one fide of a channel, you may work and navigate, buy and fell; and to the fubject on the other fide, you fhall not work or navigate, buy or fell, but under fuch reftrictions as will extinguifh the genius, and unnerve the arm of induftry; I will only fay that it ufes a language repugnant to the free fpirit of commerce, and of the Britifh and Irifh conftitution.

Great

Great eulogiums on the virtues of our people have been pronounced by some of the most respected English authors*; yet indolence is objected to them by those who discourage their industry; but they do not reflect that each of these proceeds from habit, and that the noble observation made on virtue in general is equally applicable to industry—the day that it loses its liberty half of its vigour is gone †.

The great expenditure of money by England, on account of this country, is an argument more fit for the limited views of a compting-house, than for the enlarged policy of statesmen deliberating on the general good of a great empire.

Very large sums, it is true, were advanced by England for the relief and recovery of Ireland; but these have been reimbursed fifty fold by the profits and advantages which

---

* Sir John Davis and Sir Edward Cooke.
† Νμισυ Γαρ Ἰαρεὶς ναποαιυΐαι Δαλιον ημας.
          Homer, as quoted by Longinus.

which have since arisen to England from its trade and intercourse with this kingdom. This argument may be further pursued, but accounts of mutual benefits between intimate friends and near relations should be always kept open, and every attempt to strike a balance between them tends rather to raise jealousies than to promote good will.

It has been said that the interest of England required that those restraints should be imposed. The contrary has been shewn; one of the maxims of her own law instructs us to enjoy our own property so as not to injure that of our neighbour *; and the true interest of a great country lies in the population, wealth and strength of the whole empire.

If this restrictive system was founded in justice and sound policy towards the middle and at the conclusion of the last century, the present state of the British empire requires new counsels, and a system of commerce

* Sic utere tuo, alienum non Lædas.

merce and of policy totally different from those which the circumstances of these countries, in the years 1663, 1670 and 1698, might have suggested.

But it is time to give your lordship a little relief, before I enter into a new part of my subject.

I have the honour to be,

My lord, &c.

THE
COMMERCIAL RESTRAINTS
OF
IRELAND
CONSIDERED.

EIGHTH LETTER.

THE

COMMERCIAL RESTRAINTS

OF

IRELAND

CONSIDERED.

EIGHTH LETTER.

MY LORD,
Dublin, 6th September, 1779.

BETWEEN the 23d of October, 1641, and the same day in the year 1652, five hundred and four thousand of the inhabitants of Ireland are said to have perished and been wasted by the sword, plague, famine, hardship and banishment *. If it had not been for the numbers of British which those wars had brought over †, and such who either as
adventurers

* Sir William Petty's Political Survey of Ireland, p. 19.
† Sir William Temple, 3 Vol. p. 7.

adventurers or soldiers seated themselves here on account of the satisfaction made to them in lands, the country had been by the rebellion of 1641, and the plague that followed it, nearly desolate. At the restoration almost the whole property of the kingdom was in a state of the utmost anarchy and confusion. To satisfy the clashing interests of the numerous claimants, and to determine the various and intricate disputes that arose relative to titles, required a considerable length of time. Peace and settlement, or, to use the words of one of the acts of parliament* of that time, the repairing the ruins and desolation of the kingdom were the great objects of this period.

The English law † of 1663, restraining the exportation from Ireland to America, was at that time, and for some years after, scarcely felt in this kingdom, which had then little to export except live cattle, not proper for so distant a market.

The

---

* The act of Explanation.
† 15 Ch. II.

The act of settlement passed in Ireland the year before this restrictive law, and the explanatory statute for the settlement of this kingdom, was not enacted until two years after. The country continued for a considerable time in a state of litigation, which is never favorable to industry. In 1661 the people must have been poor; the number of them of all degrees, who paid poll money in that year was about 360,000*. In 1672, when the country had greatly improved, the manufacture bestowed upon a year's exportation from Ireland, did not exceed eight thousand pounds†, and the clothing trade had not then arrived to what it had been before the last rebellion. But still the kingdom had much increased in wealth, tho' not in manufactured exports. The customs which set in 1656 for 12,000l. yearly, were in 1672 worth 80,000l. ‡ yearly, and the improvement in domestic wealth, that is to say, in building, planting, furniture, coaches,

* Sir W. Petty, p 9.
† Ib. 9. and 110.
‡ Ib. 89.

coaches, &c. is said to have advanced from 1652 to 1673 in a proportion of from one to four. Sir William Petty in the year 1672 complains not of the restraints on the exportation from Ireland to America *, but of the prohibition of exporting our cattle to England, and of our being obliged to unlade in that kingdom † the ships bound from America to Ireland; the latter regulation he considers as highly prejudicial to this country †.

The immediate object of Ireland at this time, seems to have been to get materials to employ her people at home without thinking of foreign exportations. When we advanced in the export of our woollen goods, the law of 1663 ‡, which excluded them from the American markets, must have been a great loss to this kingdom; and after we were allowed to export our linens to the British colonies in America, the restraints imposed

* Sir W. Petty, p. 9 and 10.
 Ib. 34, 71, 125.
‡ 15 Ch. II. ch. 7.

imposed by the law of 1670 upon our importations from thence became more prejudicial, and will be much more so if ever the late extension of our exports to America should under those restraints have any effect. For it is certainly a great discouragement to the carrying on trade with any country where we are allowed only to sell our manufactures and produce, but are not permitted to carry from them directly to our own country their principal manufactures or produce. The people to whom we are thus permitted to sell, want the principal inducement for dealing with us, and the great spring of commerce, which is mutual exchange, is wanting between us.

As the British legislature has thought it reasonable to extend, in a very considerable degree, our exportation to their colonies, and has doubtless intended that this favour should be useful to Ireland, it is hoped that those restraints on the importation from thence, which must render that favour of little effect, will be no longer continued.

From

From those considerations it is evident that many strong reasons respecting Ireland are now to be found against the continuance of those restrictive laws of 1663 and 1670, that did not exist at the time of making them.

The prohibition of 1699 was immediately and universally felt in this country; but in the course of human events various and powerful reasons have arisen against the continuance of that statute, which did not exist, and could not have been foreseen when it was enacted.

At the restoration the inhabitants of Ireland consisted of three different nations, English, Scotch and Irish, divided by political and religious principles, exasperated against each other by former animosities, and by present contests for property. When the settlement of the country was compleated, the people became industrious, manufactures greatly increased, and the kingdom began to flourish. The prohibition of exporting cattle to England, and, perhaps, that

of

of importing directly from America the materials of other manufactures, obliged the Irish to increase, and to manufacture their own material. They made so great a progress in both, from 1672 to 1687, that in the latter year the exports of the woollen manufacture alone amounted in value to 70,521l. 14s. 0d.

But the religious and civil animosities continued. The papists objected to the settlement of property made after the restoration *, wished to reverse the outlawries and to rescind the laws on which that settlement was founded, hoped to establish their own as the national religion, to get the power of the kingdom into their own hands, and to effect all those purposes by a king of their own religion. They endeavoured to attain all those objects by laws † passed at a meeting, which they called a parliament, held under this prince

---

* Carte, 2 Vol. 425 to 428, 465.

† Archb. Bishop King's State, 209. James the 2d in his speech from the throne in Ireland, recommended the repeal of the act of settlement.

prince after his abdication; and by their conduct at this period, as well as in the year 1642 *, shewed difpofitions unfavourable to the fubordination of Ireland to the crown of England. They could not be fuppofed to be well affected to that great Prince who defeated all their purpofes.

At the time of the revolution the numbers of our people were again very much reduced; but a great majority of the remaining inhabitants confifted of papifts. Thofe, notwithftanding their difappointment at that æra, were thought to entertain expectations of the reftoration of their popifh king, and defigns unfavorable to the eftablifhed conftitution in church and ftate. It is not to the prefent purpofe to inquire how long this

* Their demands in 1642 were the reftitution of all the plantation lands to the old inhabitants, repeal of Poyning's act, &c. Macaulay's Hift. 3 Vol. 222. In the meeting, called a parliament, held by James in Ireland, they repealed the acts of fettlement and explanation, paffed a law that the parliament of England cannot bind Ireland, and againft writs of error and appeals to England.

this difpofition prevailed. It cannot be doubted but that this was the opinion conceived of their views and principles at the time of paffing this law of the year 1699.

England could not then confider a country under fuch unfortunate circumftances as any great additional ftrength to it. Foreign proteftants were invited to fettle in it, and the emigration of papifts in great numbers to other countries was allowed, if not encouraged. Though at this period a regard to liberty as well as to œconomy, occafioned the difbanding of all the army in England, except 7000, it was thought neceffary for the fecurity of Ireland that an army of 12,000 men fhould be kept there; and for many years afterwards it was not allowed that this army fhould be recruited in this kingdom. This diftinction of parties in Ireland was in thofe times the main fpring in every movement relative to that kingdom, and affected not only political but commercial regulations. The reafon affigned by the Englifh ftatute, allowing the exportation

of

of Irish linen cloth to the plantations, is, after reciting the restrictive law of 1663*, "*yet* forasmuch as the protestant interest of "Ireland ought to be supported, by giving "the utmost encouragement to the linen "manufactures of that kingdom, in tender "regard to her majesty's good protestant "subjects of her said kingdom, be it enact- "ed," &c.

The papists, then disabled from acquiring permanent property in lands, had not the same interest with protestants in the defence of their country and in the prosperity of the British empire. But those seeds of disunion and diffidence no longer remain. No man looks now for the return of the exiled family, any more than for that of Perken Warbec; and the repeal of magna charta is as much expected as of the act of settlement. The papists, indulged with the exercise of their religious worship, and now at liberty to acquire permanent property

in

* 3d and 4th Anne, ch. 8.

in lands, are interested as well as protestants in the security and prosperity of this country; and sensible of the benign influence of our sovereign, and of the protection and happiness which they enjoy under his reign, seem to be as well affected to the king and to the constitution of the state as any other class of subjects, and at this most dangerous crisis have contributed their money to raise men for his majesty's service, and declared their readiness, had the laws permitted, to have taken arms for the defence of their country. They owe much to the favour and protection of the crown, and to the liberal and benevolent spirit of the British legislature which led the way to their relief, and they are peculiarly interested to cultivate the good opinion of their sovereign, and of their fellow-subjects in Great Britain.

The numbers of our people, since the year 1698, are more than doubled; but in point of real strength to the British empire are increased in a proportion of above eight
to

to one. In the year 1698, the numbers of our people did not much, if at all, exceed one million. Of thefe 300,000 are thought to be a liberal allowance for proteftants of all denominations. It is now fuppofed that there are not lefs in this kingdom than 2,500,000 inhabitants, loyal and affectionate fubjects to his majefty, and well-affected to the conftitution and happinefs of their country.

A political and commercial conftitution, if it could have been confidered as wifely framed for the years 1663, 1670 and 1698, ought to be reconfidered in the year 1779; what might have been good and neceffary policy in the government of one million of men difunited among themfelves, and a majority of them not to be relied upon in fupport of their king and of the laws and conftitution of their country, is bad policy in the government of two millions and a half of men now united among themfelves, and all interefted in the fupport of the crown, the laws, and the conftitution.

What

What might have been sufficient employment, and the means of acquiring a competent subsistence for one million of people, when a man by working two days in the week might have earned a sufficient support for him and his family, will never answer for two millions and a half of people*, when the hard labour of six days in the week can scarcely supply a scanty subsistence. Nor can the resources which enabled us in the last century to remit 200,000l. yearly to England †, support remittances to the amount of more than six times that sum.

Let the reasons for this restrictive system at the time of its formation be examined, and let us judge impartially, whether any one of the purposes then intended has been answered. The reasons respecting America, were to confine the Plantation-trade to England, and to make that country a storehouse of all commodities for its colonies. But

* Sir W. Petty's Survey.
† Ib. 117.

But the commercial jealoufy that has prevailed among the different ſtates of Europe, has made it difficult for any nation to keep great markets to herſelf in excluſion of the reſt of the world. It was not foreſeen at thoſe periods that the colonies, whilſt they all continued dependent, ſhould have traded with foreign nations, notwithſtanding the utmoſt efforts of Great Britain to prevent it. It was not foreſeen that thoſe colonies would have refuſed to have taken any commodities whatever from their parent country, that they ſhould afterwards have ſeparated themſelves from her empire, declared themſelves independent, refiſted her fleets and armies, obtained the moſt powerful alliances, and occaſioned the moſt dangerous and deſtructive war in which Great Britain was ever engaged. Nor could it have been foreſeen that Ireland, excluded from almoſt all direct intercourſe with them, ſhould have been nearly undone by the conteſt. The reaſons then reſpecting America no longer exiſt, and whatever may be the event of the conflict, will never exiſt to the extent expected

expected when this system of restraints and penalties was adopted.

The reasons relating to Ireland have failed also. The circumstances of this country relative to the woollen manufacture are totally changed since the year 1699. The lords and commons of England appear to have founded the law of that year on the proportion which they supposed that the charge of the woollen manufacture in England then bore to the charge of that manufacture in Ireland. In the representation from the commissioners of trade, laid before both houses †, they think it a reasonable conjecture to take the difference between both wool and labour in the two countries to be one third; and estimating on that supposition, they find that $43\frac{3}{7}$ per cent, may be laid on broad cloth exported out of Ireland, more than on the like cloth exported out of England, to bring them both to

---

† Order 14th March 1698, Lords Journ. v. 16. Eng. Com. Journs. 18th Jan. 1698, 12 v. 440.

to an equality. This muft have been an alarming reprefentation to England.

But if thofe calculations were juft at the time, which is very doubtful, the fuppofed facts on which they were founded do certainly no longer exift. Wool is now generally at a higher price in Ireland than in England, and the trifling difference in the price of labour is more than over-balanced by this and the other circumftances in favour of England, which have been before ftated; and that thofe facts fuppofed in 1698, and the inferences drawn from them, have no foundation in the prefent ftate of this country is plain from the experience of every day, which fhews that inftead of our underfelling the Englifh, they underfell us in our own markets.

Befides our exclufion from foreign markets, England had two objects in the difcouragement of our woollen trade.

It was intended that Ireland fhould fend her wool to England, and take from that country

country her woollen manufactures*. It has been already shewn that the first object has not been attained; the second has been carried so far as, for the future, to defeat its own purpose. Whilst our own manufacturers were starving for want of employment, and our wool sold for less than one half of its usual price, we have imported from England in the years 1777 and 1778 woollen goods to the enormous amount of 715,740l 13s 0d as valued at our customhouse, and of the manufactures of linen, cotton and silk mixed, to the amount of 98,086l 1s 11d, making in the whole in

those

---

* The commissioners of trade, in their representation dated the 11th November 1697, relating to the trade between England and Ireland, advise a duty to be laid upon the importation of oil, upon teasles, whether imported or *growing* there, and upon *all the utensils* employed in the making any woollen manufactures, on the utensils of worsted-combers, and particularly a duty by the yard upon all cloth and woollen stuffs, except frizes, before they are taken off the loom. Eng. Com. Journ. 12 v. 428.

those two years of distress £813,826l 14s 11d†. Between 20 and 30,000 of our manufacturers in those branches were in those two years supported by public charity. From this fact it is hoped that every reasonable man will allow the necessity of our using our own manufactures. Agreements among our people for this purpose are not, as it has been supposed, a new idea in this country. It was never so universal as at present, but has been frequently resorted to in times of distress. In the sessions of 1703, 1705 and 1707‡, the house of commons resolved unanimously, that it would greatly conduce to the relief of the poor and the good of the kingdom, that the inhabitants thereof should use none other but the manufactures of this kingdom in their apparel and the furniture of their houses; and in the last of those sessions the members engaged their honours

† See in the appendix an account of those articles imported from England into Ireland, for ten years, commencing in 1769, and ending in 1778.

‡ Com. Journ. 3 vol. 348, 548.

honours to each other, that they would conform to the faid refolution. The not importing goods from England is one of the remedies recommended by the council of trade in 1676 for alleviating fome diſtreſs that was felt at that time*; and ſir William Temple, a zealous friend to the trade and manufactures of England, recommends to lord Effex, then lord lieutenant, " to intro-
" duce as far as can be, a vein of parſimony
" throughout the country, in all things that
" are not perfectly the native growths and
" manufactures.§"

The people of England can not reaſonably object to a conduct of which they have given a memorable example‡. In 1697 the Englifh houfe of lords prefented an addrefs to king William to difcourage the ufe and wearing of all forts of furniture and cloths, not of the growth or manufac-

---

* Sir W. Petty's Political Survey, 123.
§ Sir W. Temple, 3 v. 11.
‡ Lords Journ. 16th Feb. 1697.

ture of that kingdom, and beseech him by his royal example effectually to encourage the use and wearing of all sorts of furniture and wearing cloths that are the growth of that kingdom, or manufactured there; and king William assures them that he would give the example to his subjects†, and would endeavour to make it effectually followed. The reason assigned by the lords for this address was, that the trade of the nation had suffered by the late long and expensive war. But it does not appear that there was any pressing necessity at the time, or that their manufacturers were starving for want of employment.

Common sense must discover to every man that, where foreign trade is restrained, discouraged, or prevented in any country, and where that country has the materials of manufactures, a fruitful soil, and numerous inhabitants, the home-trade is its best resource. If this is thought, by men of great knowledge, to be the most valuable of all trades,

† Lords Journ. 19th Feb. 1697.

trades §, becaufe it makes the fpeediest and the fureft returns, and becaufe it increafes at the fame time two capitals in the fame country, there is no nation on the globe, whofe wealth, population, strength and happinefs would be promoted by fuch a trade in a greater degree than ours *.

Two other reafons were affigned for this prohibition,—that the Irifh had fhewn themfelves unwilling to promote the linen manufacture †; and that there were great quantities of wool in Ireland. But they have fince cultivated the linen trade with great fuccefs, and great numbers of their people

§ See Dr. Smith's Wealth of Nations.

* The confumption of our own people is the beft and greateft market for the product and manufactures of our own country. Foreign trade is but a part of the benefit arifing from the woollen manufacture, and the leaft part; it is a fmall article in refpect to the benefit arifing to the community; and Dr. Smith affirms that all the foreign markets of England cannot be equal to one-twentieth part of her own. Dr. Smith's memoirs of wool, 2 vol. 113, 529, 530 and 556, from the Britifh merchant and Dr. Davenant.

† Addrefs of Eng. Commons, ante.

people are employed in it. Of late years, by the operation of the land-carriage bounty agriculture has increased in a degree never before known in this country; extensive tracts of lands, formerly sheep-pasture, are now under tillage, and much greater rents are given for that purpose than can be paid by stocking with sheep; the quantity of wool is greatly diminished from what it was in the year 1699, supposing it to have been then equal to the quantity in 1687*; it has been for several years lessening, and is not likely to be increased. In those two important circumstances the grounds of the apprehensions of England have ceased, and the state of Ireland has been materially altered since the year 1699.

Another reason respecting England and foreign states, particularly France, has failed. England was in 1698, in possession of the woollen trade in most of the foreign markets, and expected still to continue to supply

* King's Stat. 160, 161.

supply them, as appears by the preamble of her statute passed in that year.

She at that time expected to keep this manufacture to herself. The people of Leeds, Hallifax and Newberry † petition the house of commons, "that by some means " the woollen manufacture may be prevent- " ed from being set up in foreign countries;" and the commons in their address, mention the keeping it as much as possible *entire* to themselves. But experience has proved the vanity of those expectations; several other countries cultivate this trade with success. France now undersells her. England has lost some of those markets, and it is thought probable that Ireland, if admitted to them, might have preserved and may now recover the trade that England has lost.

A perseverance in this restrictive policy will be ruinous to the trade of Great Britain. Whatever may be the state of America, great numbers of the inhabitants of Ireland, if the circumstances of this country shall continue to be the same as at present in respect

of

† Eng. Com. Journ. 12 v. 514, 523, 528.

of trade, will emigrate there; this will give strength to that part of the empire on which Great Britain can least, and take it from that part on which at present she may most securely depend. But this is not all the mischief; those emigrants will be mostly manufacturers, and will transfer to America the woollen and linen manufactures, to the great prejudice of those trades in England, Scotland and Ireland; and then one of the means used to keep the colonies dependent, by introducing this country into a system of colonization, will be the occasion of lessening, if not dissolving, the connection between them and their parent state.

Great Britain, weakened in her extremities, should fortify the heart of her empire; Great Britain, with powerful foreign enemies united in lasting bonds against her, and with scarcely any foreign alliance to sustain her, should exert every possible effort to strengthen herself at home. The numbers of people in Ireland have more than doubled in fourscore years. How much more rapid would be the increase if the growth of the

the human race was cherished by finding sufficient employment and food for this prolific nation! it would probably double again in half a century. What a vast accession of strength such numbers of brave and active men, living almost within the sound of a trumpet, must bring to Great Britain, now said to be decreasing considerably in population! a greater certainly than double those numbers dispersed in distant parts of the globe, the expence of defending and governing of which must at all times be great. Sir W. Temple* in 1673 takes notice of the circumstances prejudicial to the trade and riches of Ireland, which had hitherto, he says, made it of more loss than value to England. They have already been mentioned. The course of time has removed some of them, and the wisdom and philantrophy of Britain may remove the rest. "Without " these circumstances, (says that honest and " able statesman,) the native fertility of the " soils and seas in so many rich commodities,

" improved

---

* 3 vol. 8.

"improved by multitudes of people and industry, with the advantage of so many excellent havens, and a situation so commodious for all sorts of foreign trade, must needs have rendered this kingdom one of the richest in Europe, and made a mighty increase both of strength and revenue to the crown of England*."

During this century Ireland has been without exaggeration, a mine of wealth to England, far beyond what any calculation has yet made it. When poor and thinly inhabited she was an expence and a burden to England; when she had acquired some proportion of riches and grew more numerous, she was one of the principal sources of her wealth. When she becomes poor again, those advantages are greatly diminished. The exports from Great Britain to Ireland in 1778† were less, that the medium value of the four preceding

* See Sir John Davis's Discourses, p. 5, 6, 194.
† Summary of imports and exports to and from Ireland, laid before the British house of commons in 1779.

preceding years in a sum of 634,444l. 3s. 0d; and in the year 1779 Great Britain is obliged, partly at her own expence, to defend this country, and for that purpose has generously bestowed out of her own exchequer a large sum of money. Those facts demonstrate that the poverty of Ireland ever has been a drain, and her riches an influx of wealth to England, to which the greater part of it will ever flow, and it imports not to that country through what channel: but the source must be cleared from obstructions, or the stream cannot continue to flow.

Such a liberal system would increase the wealth of this kingdom by means that would strengthen the hands of government, and promote the happiness of the people. Ireland would be then able to contribute largely to the support of the British empire, not only from the increase of her wealth, but from the more equal distribution of it into a greater number of hands among the various orders of the community. The present inability of Ireland arises principally from this circumstance,

circumstance, that her lower and middle classes have little or no property, and are not able, to any considerable amount, either to pay taxes, or to consume those commodities that are the usual subjects of them; and this has been the consequence of the laws which prevent trade and discourage manufactures. The same quantity of property distributed through the different classes of the people would supply resources much superior to those which can be found in the present state of Ireland*. The increase of people there under its present restraints makes but a small addition to the resources of the state in respect of taxes†. In 1685 the amount

---

* Those states are least able to pay great charge for public disbursements, whose wealth resteth chiefly in the hands of the nobility and gentry. Bac. 1 Vol. p. 10. Smith's Wealth of Nations, 2 Vol. p. 22.

† A very judicious friend of mine has, with great pains and attention, made a calculation of the numbers of people in Ireland in the year 1774, and he makes the numbers of people to amount to 2,325,041, but supposes his calculation to be under the real number. I have therefore followed the calculation commonly received, which makes their number

of the inland excife in Ireland was 75,169l. In 1762 it increafed only to 92,842l. Thofe years are taken as periods of a confiderable degree of profperity in Ireland. The people had increafed from 1685 to 1762 in a proportion of nearly 7 to 4[*], which appears from this circumftance, that in 1685 hearth money amounted to 32,659l. and in 1762 to 56,611l. At the former period the law made to reftrain and difcourage the principal trade and manufacture of Ireland had not been made. There were then vaft numbers of fheep in Ireland, and the woollen manufacture was probably in a flourifhing ftate. At the former of thofe periods the lower claffes of the people were able to confume excifable commo-

number amount to 2,500,000. He computes, as has been before mentioned, the perfons who refide in houfes of one hearth, to be 1,877,220. Thofe find it very difficult to pay hearth-money, and are thought to be unable to pay any other taxes. If this is fo, according to this calculation, there are but 447,821 people in Ireland able to pay taxes.

[*] Ireland was much more numerous in 1685 than at any time, after the revolution, during that century, there having been a great wafte of people in the rebellion at that era.

commodities. In the latter they lived for the moſt part on the immediate produce of the ſoil. The numbers of people in a ſtate, like thoſe of a private family, if the individuals have the means of acquiring, add to the wealth, and if they have not thoſe means, to the poverty of the community. Population is not always a proof of the proſperity of a nation; the people may be very numerous, and very poor and wretched. A temperate climate, fruitful ſoil, bays and rivers well ſtocked with fiſh, the habits of life among the lower claſſes, and a long peace, are ſufficient to increaſe the numbers of people; theſe are the true wealth of every ſtate that has wiſdom to encourage the induſtry of its inhabitants, and a country which ſupplies in abundance the materials for that induſtry. If the ſtate, or the family ſhould diſcourage induſtry, and not allow one of the family to work, becauſe another is of the ſame trade, the conſequences to the great or the little community, muſt be equally fatal.

Is

Is there not bufinefs enough in this great world for the people of two adjoining iflands without depreffing the inhabitants of one of them? let the magnanimity and philanthrophy of Great Britain addrefs her poor fifter kingdom in the fame language which the good-natured uncle Toby ufes to the fly, in fetting it at liberty—" poor fly, there's room enough for thee and me!"

I have the honour to be,

My Lord, &c.

THE COMMERCIAL RESTRAINTS

OF

IRELAND

CONSIDERED.

NINTH LETTER.

Q

THE COMMERCIAL RESTRAINTS OF IRELAND CONSIDERED.

NINTH LETTER.

My Lord,

Dublin, 10th Sept. 1779.

BESIDES those already mentioned, various other commercial restraints and prohibitions give the British trader and manufacturer many great and important advantages over the Irish. Whilst our markets are at all times open to all their productions and manufactures, with inconsiderable duties on the import, their markets are open or shut against us as suits their conveniency. On several articles of the first importance, and on almost all our own manufactures, imported into Great Britain, duties are imposed equal to a prohibition. In the instance of woollen-goods, their's in our ports pay but a small duty, our's in their ports are loaded with duties *, which amount to a prohibition †; their's on the exportation are subject to no duty; our's, if permitted to be exported, would, as the law now stands, be subject to a duty ‡ over and above that payable for alnage and for the alnager's fee. If the act of 1699 was repealed, the English would still have many great advantages over us in the woollen trade.

In our staple manufacture, the bounties given on the exportation of white and brown Irish

---

* 12th Ch. II. ch. 4. Eng.

† Yet in favour of Great Britain, old and new drapery imported into Ireland from other countries are subject to duties equal to a prohibition. Ir. act 14th and 15th Ch. II. ch. 8.

‡ On every piece of old drapery exported, containing 36 yards, and so for a greater or lesser quantity 3s. 4d. and of new drapery 9d. for the subsidy of alnage and alnager's fee. See 17th and 18th Ch. II. ch. 15. Ir. But the English have taken off these and all other duties from their manufactures made or mixed with wool. Eng. act 11 and 12 W. III. ch. 20.

Irish linen from Great-Britain would still continue that trade in the hands of the British merchant. On all coloured linens a duty* equal to a prohibition is imposed on the importation into Great-Britain; but their's imported to us are subject † to ten per cent, and under that duty they have imported considerably. This inequality of duty and the bounty given by the British act of the tenth of Geo. the 3d on the exportation of their chequered and striped linens from Great-Britain, secures to them the continuance of the great superiority which they have acquired over us in those very valuable branches of this trade. In many other articles they have given themselves great advantages. Beer they export to us in such quantities as almost to ruin our brewery; but they prevent our exportation to them by duties, laid on the import there, equal to a prohibition. Of malt they make large exports to us, to the prejudice of our agriculture, but have

absolutely

---

* Thirty per cent. by the British acts of 9 and 10 Anne, ch. 39, and 12 Anne, ch. 9.

† This tax is ad valorem, and the linen not valued.

abſolutely prohibited our exportation of that commodity to them. Some manufactures they retain ſolely to themſelves, which we are prohibited from exporting, and cannot import from any country but Great Britain, as glaſs of all kinds. Hops they do not allow us to import from any other place, and in a facetious ſtyle of interdiction pronounce ſuch importation to be a common nuiſance*. They go further, and by laying a duty on the export, and denying the draw-back, oblige the Iriſh conſumer to pay a tax appropriated, it is ſaid, to the payment of a Britiſh debt. I ſhall make no political, but the ſubject requires a commercial obſervation—it is this—the man who keeps a market ſolely to himſelf in excluſion of all others, whether he appears as buyer † or ſeller, fixes his own price, and becomes the arbiter of the profit and loſs of every cuſtomer.

The

---

* Brit. Act, 9 Ann, ch. 12.

† Hence it is that the price of wool in England is ſaid to be 50 per cent. below the market price of Europe, Smith's Memoirs of wool.

The various manufactures * made or mixed with cotton, are subject by several British acts to duties on the importation, amounting to 25 per cent.

By another act, penalties † are imposed on wearing any of those manufactures in Great-Britain, unless made in that country. Those laws have effectually excluded the Irish manufactures in all those branches from the British markets; and it has been already shewn, that they cannot be sent to the American. From Great Britain into Ireland all those articles are imported in immense quantities, being subject here to duties amounting to ten per cent. only.

But it would be tedious to descend into a further detail, and disgusting to write a book of rates instead of a letter ‡.

---

* 12 Ch. II. ch. 5. 3 and 4 Ann. ch. 4. 4 and 5 W. and M. ch. 5.

† 7 G. 1. ch. 7.

‡ When the commercial restraints of Ireland are the subject, a source of occasional and ruinous restrictions ought not

Their superior capitals and expertness, give them decisive advantages in every species of trade and manufacture. By the extension of the commerce of Ireland, Great Britain would acquire new and important advantages, not only by the wealth it would bring to that country, and the encrease of strength to the empire, but by opening to the British merchant new sources of trade from Ireland.

It is time to draw to a conclusion. I have reviewed my letters to your lordship for the purpose of avoiding every possible occasion of offence; I flatter myself every reader will discern that they have been written with upright and friendly intentions, not to excite jealousies but to remove prejudices, to moderate and conciliate, and that they are intended as an appeal, not to the passions of the multitude, but to the wisdom, justice and generosity of Britain. Shakespeare could place

not to be passed over. Since the year 1740, there have been 24 embargoes in Ireland, one of which lasted three years.

place a tongue in every wound of Cæfar; but Antony meant to inflame; and the only purpofe of thofe letters is to perfuade. I have therefore not even removed the mantle, except where neceffity required it.

In extraordinary cafes where the facts are ftronger than the voice of the pleader, it is not unufual to allow the client to fpeak for himfelf. Will you, my lord, one of the leading advocates for Ireland, allow her to addrefs her elder fifter, and to ftate her own cafe; not in the ftrains of paffion or refentment, nor in the tone of remonftrance, but with a modeft enumeration of unexaggerated facts in pathetic fimplicity; fhe will tell her, with a countenance full of affection and tendernefs, " I have received from you invalua-
" ble gifts, the law of * common right, your
" great charter, and the fundamentals of your
" conftitution. The temple of liberty in
" your country, has been frequently fortifi-
" ed, improved and embellifhed; mine erect-
" ed

* The common law of England.

" ed many centuries since the perfect mo-
" del of your own; you will not suffer me
" to strengthen, secure, or repair; firm and
" well cemented as it is, it must moulder un-
" der the hand of Time for want of that at-
" tention, which is due to the venerable
" fabrick*. We are connected by the strong-
" est ties of natural affection, common secu-
" rity, and a long interchange of the kindest
" offices on both sides. But for more than a
" century you have, in some instances, mis-
" taken our mutual interest. I sent you my
" herds and my flocks, filled your people
" with abundance, and gave them leisure
" to attend to more profitable pursuits, than
" the humble employment of shepherds and
" of herds-men. But you rejected my pro-
" duce †, and reprobated this intercourse in
" terms the most opprobrious. I submitted;
" the temporary loss was mine, but the per-
" petual

---

* Heads of bills for passing into a law the habeas corpus act, and that for making the tenure of judges during good behaviour, have repeatedly passed the Irish house of commons, but were not returned.

† The Eng. act of Ch. II. ch. calls the importation of cattle from Ireland, a common nusance.

"petual prejudice your own. I incited my
"children to induſtry, and gave them my
"principal materials to manufacture. Their
"honeſt labours were attended with mode-
"rate ſucceſs, but ſufficient to awaken the
"commercial jealouſy of ſome of your ſons;
"indulging their groundleſs apprehenſions,
"you deſired my materials and diſcouraged
"the induſtry of my people. I complied
"with your wiſhes, and gave to your chil-
"dren the bread of my own; but the ene-
"mies of our race were the gainers; they
"applied themſelves with tenfold encreaſe
"to thoſe purſuits which were reſtrained in
"my people, who would have added to the
"wealth and ſtrength of your empire what
"by this fatal error you transfered to fo-
"reign nations. You held out another ob-
"ject to me with promiſes of the utmoſt
"encouragement. I wanted the means, but
"I obtained them from other countries, and
"have long cultivated, at great expence and
"with the moſt unremitted efforts, that
"ſpecies of induſtry which you recommend-
"ed. You ſoon united with another great
                                    "family,

" family, engaged in the same pursuit,
" which you were also obliged to encourage
" among them, and afterwards embarked in
" it yourself, and became my rival in that
" which you had destined for my principal
" support. This support is now become
" inadequate to the encreased number of
" my offspring, many of whom want the
" means of subsistence. My ports are ever
" hospitably open for your reception, and
" shut, whenever your interest requires it,
" against all others; but your's are in many
" instances barred against me, with your
" dominions in Asia, Africa and America;
" my sons were long deprived of all benefi-
" cial intercourse, and yet to those colonies
" I transported my treasures for the payment
" of your armies, and in a war waged
" for their defence, one hundred thousand
" of my sons fought by your side[*]. Con-
" quest attended our arms. You gained a
" great increase of empire and of commerce;
                                    " and

[*] This number of Irishmen was computed to have served in the fleets and armies of Great Britain during the last
war.

" and my people a further extension of re-
" straints and prohibitions†. In those ef-
" forts I have exhausted my strength, mort-
" gaged my territories, and am now sinking
" under the pressure of enormous debts con-
" tracted from my zealous attachment to
" your interests, to the extension of your
" empire and the encrease of your glory.
" By the present unhappy war for the reco-
" very of those colonies, from which they
" were long excluded, my children are re-
" duced to the lowest ebb of poverty and
" distress. It is true, you have lately with
" the kindest intentions, allowed me an ex-
" tensive liberty of selling to the inhabitants
" of those parts of your empire, but they
" have no inducement to buy, because I can-
" not take their produce in return. Your
" liberality has opened a new fountain, but
" your

† The Furs of Canada, the Indigo of Florida, the sugars of Dominica, St. Vincent's and the Grenades, with every other valuable production of those acquisitions, Ireland was prohibited to receive but through another channel. Her poverty scarcely gathered a crum from the sumptuous table of her sister.

" your caution will not fuffer me to draw
" from it. The ftream of commerce, intend-
" ed to refresh the exhaufted ftrength of my
" children, flies untafted from their parched
" lips.

" The common parent of all has been e-
" qually beneficent to us both. We both
" poffefs in great abundance the means
" of induftry and of happinefs. My fields
" are not lefs fertile, nor my harbours lefs
" numerous than your's. My fons are not
" lefs renowned than your own for valour,
" juftice and generofity. Many of them
" are your defcendants, and have fome of
" your beft blood in their veins. But the
" narrow policy of man has counteracted
" the inftincts and the bounties of nature.
" In the midft of thofe fertile fields, fome of
" my children perifh before my eyes for want
" of food, and others fly for refuge to hof-
" tile nations.

" Suffer

"Suffer no longer, respected sister, the
"narrow jealousy of commerce to mislead
"the wisdom and to impair the strength of
"the state. Encrease my resources, they
"shall be your's, my riches and strength, my
"poverty and weakness will become your
"own. What a triumph to our enemies,
"and what an affliction to me, in the pre-
"sent distracted circumstances of the em-
"pire, to see my people reduced, by the
"necessity of avoiding famine, to the reso-
"lution of traficking almost solely with
"themselves! great and powerful enemies
"are combined against you, many of your
"distant connections have deserted you,
"encrease your strength at home, open
"and extend the numerous resources of my
"country, of which you have not hitherto
"availed yourself or allowed me the benefit.
"Our encreased force and the full exertions
"of our strength will be the most effectual
"means of resisting the combination formed
"against you by foreign enemies and distant
                                        "subjects,

"subjects, and of giving new lustre to our "crowns, and happiness and contentment to "our people."

THE END.

	New.
	Quantity.
1769	394553
1770	462499
1771	362096
1772	314703
1773	387143
1774	461407
1775	465611
1776	676485
1777	731819
1778	741426

Years ending the 25th of March

APPENDIX. No. III.

An Account of the Quantity of Linen Cloth exported out of Ireland to Great-Britain and Plantations, prior to the Year 1743.

	Linen Cloth exported to Great-Britain. Yards.	Linen Cloth exported to Plantations. Yards.
1705	739,278	19,742
1706	1,325,771	62,727
1707	1,847,564	81,037
1708	343,359	29,606
1709	1,539,250	113,939
1710	1,528,185	136,844
1711	1,131,629	89,262
1712	1,320,968	43,011

Since thefe papers were fent to the prefs, the Commons of Ireland have, in their addrefs to his majefty, refolved unanimoufly, " that it is not by temporary expedients, " but by a free trade alone that this nation " is now to be faved from impending ruin". And the lords have in their addrefs unanimoufly entered into a refolution of the fame import.

www.ingramcontent.com/pod-product-compliance
Lightning Source LLC
Chambersburg PA
CBHW032205230426
43672CB00011B/2520